7 A.M. Journal

Affirmations & Manifestations

7 A.M.

=

7 Affirmations & Manifestations

1. I A.M. Happy
2. I A.M. Healthy
3. I A.M. Wealthy
4. I A.M. Successful
5. I A.M. Grateful
6. I A.M. Limitless
7. I A.M. Loved

7

is the number of completeness

and perfection.

This journal is a reminder to tell

you that you are

100% worthy

and whole.

You are God's creation, and

He doesn't make mistakes.

You're a complete masterpiece

all by yourself and you do not

need anyone else to validate

your existence.

DEDICATED TO *You*

I hope this journal brings you clarity, guidance, strength, and peace on your journey. Nothing is greater than knowing your worth and understanding that It all starts with YOU!

With daily affirmations and elevating your mindset, you can manifest whatever your heart desires. Applying daily affirmations and manifestations will help you manifest the life you want now. You were created for greatness!

Believe in yourself!

Now let's get started.

7 AFFIRMATIONS for Success

1. I am creative and smart
2. I am focused and determined
3. I am wealthy and money is overflowing in my life
4. I am attracting positive situations
5. I am capable of creating success
6. I am creating the life of my dreams
7. I am grateful for all that I am accomplishing

7

7 AFFIRMATIONS for Good Health

1. I am healthy

2. I am strong

3. I am filled with energy

4. I am in love with my body

5. I am in the best shape of my life

6. I am capable of doing amazing things

7. I choose happiness and love for myself and others.

7 AFFIRMATIONS

for

Self Love

1. I am beautiful

2. I am loved

3. I am appreciated

4. I am enough

5. I am confident

6. I am a positive light

7. I am worthy of a great life

7 AFFIRMATIONS for Friends & Family

1. I am grateful for my family

2. I am grateful for my friends

3. I am grateful to have a strong and healthy relationship with my family and friends

4. I am grateful that my family and friends support me

5. I am grateful that my family and friends are healthy

6. I am grateful for the quality time I'm able to spend with my family and friends

7. I am grateful that my family and friends are blessed with abundance

7 TYPES OF NEGATIVITY that can *Stop* MANIFESTATIONS

1. Doubt
2. Lack of faith
3. Jealousy
4. Unforgivness
5. Impatience
6. Negative conversations
7. Not controlling your thoughts

Remember the energy you put out is what you get back.

Speak and think positive!

7 FAVE Bible VERSES

Proverbs 3:5-6

Trust in the Lord with all your heart and lean not on your own understanding; in all your ways submit to him, and he will make your paths straight.

Philippians 4:13

I Can Do All Things Through Christ Who Strengthens Me

Romans 12:12

Be joyful in hope, patient in affliction, faithful in prayer.

Psalm 107:1

Give thanks to the LORD, for he is good; his love endures forever.

Jeremiah 29:11

For I know the plans I have for you," declares the LORD, "plans to prosper you and not to harm you, plans to give you hope and a future.

Mathew 11:28

Come to me, all you who are weary and burdened, and I will give you rest.

Psalm 16:8

I keep my eyes always on the LORD. With him at my right hand, I will not be shaken

Whatever has happened,
happened for a reason.
Leave the past in the past.
Give energy to what matters and
what you want to manifest

Now

NEW YEAR NEW GOALS!

MY *Goals* FOR 2021

ACTIONS STEPS

New thoughts can open up a new
world of possibilities for you,

elevate

your mindset.

____ /____ /____

COUNT YOUR BLESSINGS!

LIST 7 THINGS YOU ARE *grateful* FOR

Today I A.M. Grateful for

1. ______________________________

Because: ______________________________

____

2. ______________________________

Because: ______________________________

____

3. ______________________________

Because: ______________________________

____

4. ______________________________

Because: ______________________________

____

5. ______________________________

Because: ______________________________

____

6. ______________________________

Because: ______________________________

____

7. ______________________________

Because: ______________________________

____

Once you finish, go back and read everything and say to yourself or out loud: "Thank You God for this blessing" after each blessing. Having an attitude of gratitude will attract more to be grateful for in your life.

____ /____ /____

COUNT YOUR BLESSINGS!

LIST 7 THINGS YOU ARE *grateful* FOR

Today I A.M. Grateful for

1. ______________________________

Because: ______________________________

____

2. ______________________________

Because: ______________________________

____

3. ______________________________

Because: ______________________________

____

4. ______________________________

Because: ______________________________

____

5. ______________________________

Because: ______________________________

____

6. ______________________________

Because: ______________________________

____

7. ______________________________

Because: ______________________________

____

Once you finish, go back and read everything and say to yourself or out loud: "Thank You God for this blessing" after each blessing. Having an attitude of gratitude will attract more to be grateful for in your life.

____ / ____ / ____

COUNT YOUR BLESSINGS!

LIST 7 THINGS YOU ARE *grateful* FOR

Today I A.M. Grateful for

1. ______________________

Because: ______________________

____

2. ______________________

Because: ______________________

____

3. ______________________

Because: ______________________

____

4. ______________________

Because: ______________________

____

5. ______________________

Because: ______________________

____

6. ______________________

Because: ______________________

____

7. ______________________

Because: ______________________

____

Once you finish, go back and read everything and say to yourself or out loud: "Thank You God for this blessing" after each blessing. Having an attitude of gratitude will attract more to be grateful for in your life.

____ / ____ / ____

COUNT YOUR BLESSINGS!

LIST 7 THINGS YOU ARE *grateful* FOR

Today I A.M. Grateful for

1. ______

Because: ______

______

2. ______

Because: ______

______

3. ______

Because: ______

______

4. ______

Because: ______

______

5. ______

Because: ______

______

6. ______

Because: ______

______

7. ______

Because: ______

______

Once you finish, go back and read everything and say to yourself or out loud: "Thank You God for this blessing" after each blessing. Having an attitude of gratitude will attract more to be grateful for in your life.

____ / ____ / ____

COUNT YOUR BLESSINGS!

LIST 7 THINGS YOU ARE *grateful* FOR

Today I A.M. Grateful for

1. ______________________________

Because: ______________________________

____

2. ______________________________

Because: ______________________________

____

3. ______________________________

Because: ______________________________

____

4. ______________________________

Because: ______________________________

____

5. ______________________________

Because: ______________________________

____

6. ______________________________

Because: ______________________________

____

7. ______________________________

Because: ______________________________

____

Once you finish, go back and read everything and say to yourself or out loud: "Thank You God for this blessing" after each blessing. Having an attitude of gratitude will attract more to be grateful for in your life.

____ /____ /____

COUNT YOUR BLESSINGS!

LIST 7 THINGS YOU ARE *grateful* FOR

Today I A.M. Grateful for

1. ________________________________

Because: ________________________________

____

2. ________________________________

Because: ________________________________

____

3. ________________________________

Because: ________________________________

____

4. ________________________________

Because: ________________________________

____

5. ________________________________

Because: ________________________________

____

6. ________________________________

Because: ________________________________

____

7. ________________________________

Because: ________________________________

____

Once you finish, go back and read everything and say to yourself or out loud: "Thank You God for this blessing" after each blessing. Having an attitude of gratitude will attract more to be grateful for in your life.

____ /____ /____

COUNT YOUR BLESSINGS!

LIST 7 THINGS YOU ARE *grateful* FOR

Today I A.M. Grateful for

1. ____________________

Because: ____________________

____

2. ____________________

Because: ____________________

____

3. ____________________

Because: ____________________

____

4. ____________________

Because: ____________________

____

5. ____________________

Because: ____________________

____

6. ____________________

Because: ____________________

____

7. ____________________

Because: ____________________

____

Once you finish, go back and read everything and say to yourself or out loud: "Thank You God for this blessing" after each blessing. Having an attitude of gratitude will attract more to be grateful for in your life.

____ / ____ / ____

COUNT YOUR BLESSINGS!

LIST 7 THINGS YOU ARE *grateful* FOR

Today I A.M. Grateful for

1. ______________________________

Because: ______________________________

____

2. ______________________________

Because: ______________________________

____

3. ______________________________

Because: ______________________________

____

4. ______________________________

Because: ______________________________

____

5. ______________________________

Because: ______________________________

____

6. ______________________________

Because: ______________________________

____

7. ______________________________

Because: ______________________________

____

Once you finish, go back and read everything and say to yourself or out loud: "Thank You God for this blessing" after each blessing. Having an attitude of gratitude will attract more to be grateful for in your life.

____ /____ /____

COUNT YOUR BLESSINGS!

LIST 7 THINGS YOU ARE *grateful* FOR

Today I A.M. Grateful for

1. ______________________________

Because: ______________________________

____

2. ______________________________

Because: ______________________________

____

3. ______________________________

Because: ______________________________

____

4. ______________________________

Because: ______________________________

____

5. ______________________________

Because: ______________________________

____

6. ______________________________

Because: ______________________________

____

7. ______________________________

Because: ______________________________

____

Once you finish, go back and read everything and say to yourself or out loud: "Thank You God for this blessing" after each blessing. Having an attitude of gratitude will attract more to be grateful for in your life.

____ /____ /____

COUNT YOUR BLESSINGS!

LIST 7 THINGS YOU ARE *grateful* FOR

Today I A.M. Grateful for

1. ______________________________

Because: ______________________________

____

2. ______________________________

Because: ______________________________

____

3. ______________________________

Because: ______________________________

____

4. ______________________________

Because: ______________________________

____

5. ______________________________

Because: ______________________________

____

6. ______________________________

Because: ______________________________

____

7. ______________________________

Because: ______________________________

____

Once you finish, go back and read everything and say to yourself or out loud: "Thank You God for this blessing" after each blessing. Having an attitude of gratitude will attract more to be grateful for in your life.

____ / ____ / ____

COUNT YOUR BLESSINGS!

LIST 7 THINGS YOU ARE *grateful* FOR

Today I A.M. Grateful for

1. ______________________________

Because: ______________________________

____

2. ______________________________

Because: ______________________________

____

3. ______________________________

Because: ______________________________

____

4. ______________________________

Because: ______________________________

____

5. ______________________________

Because: ______________________________

____

6. ______________________________

Because: ______________________________

____

7. ______________________________

Because: ______________________________

____

Once you finish, go back and read everything and say to yourself or out loud: "Thank You God for this blessing" after each blessing. Having an attitude of gratitude will attract more to be grateful for in your life.

____ / ____ / ____

COUNT YOUR BLESSINGS!

LIST 7 THINGS YOU ARE *grateful* FOR

Today I A.M. Grateful for

1. ____

Because: ____

____

2. ____

Because: ____

____

3. ____

Because: ____

____

4. ____

Because: ____

____

5. ____

Because: ____

____

6. ____

Because: ____

____

7. ____

Because: ____

____

Once you finish, go back and read everything and say to yourself or out loud: "Thank You God for this blessing" after each blessing. Having an attitude of gratitude will attract more to be grateful for in your life.

____ /____ /____

COUNT YOUR BLESSINGS!

LIST 7 THINGS YOU ARE *grateful* FOR

Today I A.M. Grateful for

1. ______________________________

Because: ______________________________

____

2. ______________________________

Because: ______________________________

____

3. ______________________________

Because: ______________________________

____

4. ______________________________

Because: ______________________________

____

5. ______________________________

Because: ______________________________

____

6. ______________________________

Because: ______________________________

____

7. ______________________________

Because: ______________________________

____

Once you finish, go back and read everything and say to yourself or out loud: "Thank You God for this blessing" after each blessing. Having an attitude of gratitude will attract more to be grateful for in your life.

____ / ____ / ____

COUNT YOUR BLESSINGS!

LIST 7 THINGS YOU ARE *grateful* FOR

Today I A.M. Grateful for

1. ______________________________

Because: ______________________________

____

2. ______________________________

Because: ______________________________

____

3. ______________________________

Because: ______________________________

____

4. ______________________________

Because: ______________________________

____

5. ______________________________

Because: ______________________________

____

6. ______________________________

Because: ______________________________

____

7. ______________________________

Because: ______________________________

____

Once you finish, go back and read everything and say to yourself or out loud: "Thank You God for this blessing" after each blessing. Having an attitude of gratitude will attract more to be grateful for in your life.

____ / ____ / ____

COUNT YOUR BLESSINGS!

LIST 7 THINGS YOU ARE *grateful* FOR

Today I A.M. Grateful for

1. ________________________________

Because: ________________________________

____

2. ________________________________

Because: ________________________________

____

3. ________________________________

Because: ________________________________

____

4. ________________________________

Because: ________________________________

____

5. ________________________________

Because: ________________________________

____

6. ________________________________

Because: ________________________________

____

7. ________________________________

Because: ________________________________

____

Once you finish, go back and read everything and say to yourself or out loud: "Thank You God for this blessing" after each blessing. Having an attitude of gratitude will attract more to be grateful for in your life.

____ / ____ / ____

COUNT YOUR BLESSINGS!

LIST 7 THINGS YOU ARE *grateful* FOR

Today I A.M. Grateful for

1. ______________________________

Because: ______________________________

____

2. ______________________________

Because: ______________________________

____

3. ______________________________

Because: ______________________________

____

4. ______________________________

Because: ______________________________

____

5. ______________________________

Because: ______________________________

____

6. ______________________________

Because: ______________________________

____

7. ______________________________

Because: ______________________________

____

Once you finish, go back and read everything and say to yourself or out loud: "Thank You God for this blessing" after each blessing. Having an attitude of gratitude will attract more to be grateful for in your life.

____ / ____ / ____

COUNT YOUR BLESSINGS!

LIST 7 THINGS YOU ARE *grateful* FOR

Today I A.M. Grateful for

1. ______________________________

Because: ______________________________

____

2. ______________________________

Because: ______________________________

____

3. ______________________________

Because: ______________________________

____

4. ______________________________

Because: ______________________________

____

5. ______________________________

Because: ______________________________

____

6. ______________________________

Because: ______________________________

____

7. ______________________________

Because: ______________________________

____

Once you finish, go back and read everything and say to yourself or out loud: "Thank You God for this blessing" after each blessing. Having an attitude of gratitude will attract more to be grateful for in your life.

____ / ____ / ____

COUNT YOUR BLESSINGS!

LIST 7 THINGS YOU ARE *grateful* FOR

Today I A.M. Grateful for

1. ____________________

Because: ____________________

____

2. ____________________

Because: ____________________

____

3. ____________________

Because: ____________________

____

4. ____________________

Because: ____________________

____

5. ____________________

Because: ____________________

____

6. ____________________

Because: ____________________

____

7. ____________________

Because: ____________________

____

Once you finish, go back and read everything and say to yourself or out loud: "Thank You God for this blessing" after each blessing. Having an attitude of gratitude will attract more to be grateful for in your life.

____ / ____ / ____

COUNT YOUR BLESSINGS!

LIST 7 THINGS YOU ARE *grateful* FOR

Today I A.M. Grateful for

1. ______________________________

Because: ______________________________

____

2. ______________________________

Because: ______________________________

____

3. ______________________________

Because: ______________________________

____

4. ______________________________

Because: ______________________________

____

5. ______________________________

Because: ______________________________

____

6. ______________________________

Because: ______________________________

____

7. ______________________________

Because: ______________________________

____

Once you finish, go back and read everything and say to yourself or out loud: "Thank You God for this blessing" after each blessing. Having an attitude of gratitude will attract more to be grateful for in your life.

____ /____ /____

COUNT YOUR BLESSINGS!

LIST 7 THINGS YOU ARE *grateful* FOR

Today I A.M. Grateful for

1. ______________________________

Because: ______________________________

____

2. ______________________________

Because: ______________________________

____

3. ______________________________

Because: ______________________________

____

4. ______________________________

Because: ______________________________

____

5. ______________________________

Because: ______________________________

____

6. ______________________________

Because: ______________________________

____

7. ______________________________

Because: ______________________________

____

Once you finish, go back and read everything and say to yourself or out loud: "Thank You God for this blessing" after each blessing. Having an attitude of gratitude will attract more to be grateful for in your life.

____ / ____ / ____

COUNT YOUR BLESSINGS!

LIST 7 THINGS YOU ARE *grateful* FOR

Today I A.M. Grateful for

1. ____________________

Because: ____________________

2. ____________________

Because: ____________________

3. ____________________

Because: ____________________

4. ____________________

Because: ____________________

5. ____________________

Because: ____________________

6. ____________________

Because: ____________________

7. ____________________

Because: ____________________

Once you finish, go back and read everything and say to yourself or out loud: “Thank You God for this blessing” after each blessing. Having an attitude of gratitude will attract more to be grateful for in your life.

____ / ____ / ____

COUNT YOUR BLESSINGS!

LIST 7 THINGS YOU ARE *grateful* FOR

Today I A.M. Grateful for

1. ______________________________

Because: ______________________________

____

2. ______________________________

Because: ______________________________

____

3. ______________________________

Because: ______________________________

____

4. ______________________________

Because: ______________________________

____

5. ______________________________

Because: ______________________________

____

6. ______________________________

Because: ______________________________

____

7. ______________________________

Because: ______________________________

____

Once you finish, go back and read everything and say to yourself or out loud: "Thank You God for this blessing" after each blessing. Having an attitude of gratitude will attract more to be grateful for in your life.

____ / ____ / ____

COUNT YOUR BLESSINGS!

LIST 7 THINGS YOU ARE *grateful* FOR

Today I A.M. Grateful for

1. ______________________________

Because: ______________________________

____

2. ______________________________

Because: ______________________________

____

3. ______________________________

Because: ______________________________

____

4. ______________________________

Because: ______________________________

____

5. ______________________________

Because: ______________________________

____

6. ______________________________

Because: ______________________________

____

7. ______________________________

Because: ______________________________

____

Once you finish, go back and read everything and say to yourself or out loud: "Thank You God for this blessing" after each blessing. Having an attitude of gratitude will attract more to be grateful for in your life.

____ / ____ / ____

COUNT YOUR BLESSINGS!

LIST 7 THINGS YOU ARE *grateful* FOR

Today I A.M. Grateful for

1. ______________________________

Because: ______________________________

____

2. ______________________________

Because: ______________________________

____

3. ______________________________

Because: ______________________________

____

4. ______________________________

Because: ______________________________

____

5. ______________________________

Because: ______________________________

____

6. ______________________________

Because: ______________________________

____

7. ______________________________

Because: ______________________________

____

Once you finish, go back and read everything and say to yourself or out loud: "Thank You God for this blessing" after each blessing. Having an attitude of gratitude will attract more to be grateful for in your life.

____ / ____ / ____

COUNT YOUR BLESSINGS!

LIST 7 THINGS YOU ARE *grateful* FOR

Today I A.M. Grateful for

1. ______________________________

Because: ______________________________

____

2. ______________________________

Because: ______________________________

____

3. ______________________________

Because: ______________________________

____

4. ______________________________

Because: ______________________________

____

5. ______________________________

Because: ______________________________

____

6. ______________________________

Because: ______________________________

____

7. ______________________________

Because: ______________________________

____

Once you finish, go back and read everything and say to yourself or out loud: "Thank You God for this blessing" after each blessing. Having an attitude of gratitude will attract more to be grateful for in your life.

____ / ____ / ____

COUNT YOUR BLESSINGS!

LIST 7 THINGS YOU ARE *grateful* FOR

Today I A.M. Grateful for

1. ____________________

Because: ____________________

2. ____________________

Because: ____________________

3. ____________________

Because: ____________________

4. ____________________

Because: ____________________

5. ____________________

Because: ____________________

6. ____________________

Because: ____________________

7. ____________________

Because: ____________________

Once you finish, go back and read everything and say to yourself or out loud: "Thank You God for this blessing" after each blessing. Having an attitude of gratitude will attract more to be grateful for in your life.

____ / ____ / ____

COUNT YOUR BLESSINGS!

LIST 7 THINGS YOU ARE *grateful* FOR

Today I A.M. Grateful for

1. ____________________

Because: ____________________

____

2. ____________________

Because: ____________________

____

3. ____________________

Because: ____________________

____

4. ____________________

Because: ____________________

____

5. ____________________

Because: ____________________

____

6. ____________________

Because: ____________________

____

7. ____________________

Because: ____________________

____

Once you finish, go back and read everything and say to yourself or out loud: "Thank You God for this blessing" after each blessing. Having an attitude of gratitude will attract more to be grateful for in your life.

____ /____ /____

COUNT YOUR BLESSINGS!

LIST 7 THINGS YOU ARE *grateful* FOR

Today I A.M. Grateful for

1. ______________________________

Because: ______________________________

____

2. ______________________________

Because: ______________________________

____

3. ______________________________

Because: ______________________________

____

4. ______________________________

Because: ______________________________

____

5. ______________________________

Because: ______________________________

____

6. ______________________________

Because: ______________________________

____

7. ______________________________

Because: ______________________________

____

Once you finish, go back and read everything and say to yourself or out loud: "Thank You God for this blessing" after each blessing. Having an attitude of gratitude will attract more to be grateful for in your life.

____ / ____ / ____

COUNT YOUR BLESSINGS!

LIST 7 THINGS YOU ARE *grateful* FOR

Today I A.M. Grateful for

1. ______________________________

Because: ______________________________

____

2. ______________________________

Because: ______________________________

____

3. ______________________________

Because: ______________________________

____

4. ______________________________

Because: ______________________________

____

5. ______________________________

Because: ______________________________

____

6. ______________________________

Because: ______________________________

____

7. ______________________________

Because: ______________________________

____

Once you finish, go back and read everything and say to yourself or out loud: "Thank You God for this blessing" after each blessing. Having an attitude of gratitude will attract more to be grateful for in your life.

____ /____ /____

COUNT YOUR BLESSINGS!

LIST 7 THINGS YOU ARE *grateful* FOR

Today I A.M. Grateful for

1. ______________________________

Because: ______________________________

____

2. ______________________________

Because: ______________________________

____

3. ______________________________

Because: ______________________________

____

4. ______________________________

Because: ______________________________

____

5. ______________________________

Because: ______________________________

____

6. ______________________________

Because: ______________________________

____

7. ______________________________

Because: ______________________________

____

Once you finish, go back and read everything and say to yourself or out loud: "Thank You God for this blessing" after each blessing. Having an attitude of gratitude will attract more to be grateful for in your life.

____ / ____ / ____

COUNT YOUR BLESSINGS!

LIST 7 THINGS YOU ARE *grateful* FOR

Today I A.M. Grateful for

1. ____________________

Because: ____________________

____

2. ____________________

Because: ____________________

____

3. ____________________

Because: ____________________

____

4. ____________________

Because: ____________________

____

5. ____________________

Because: ____________________

____

6. ____________________

Because: ____________________

____

7. ____________________

Because: ____________________

____

Once you finish, go back and read everything and say to yourself or out loud: "Thank You God for this blessing" after each blessing. Having an attitude of gratitude will attract more to be grateful for in your life.

____ / ____ / ____

COUNT YOUR BLESSINGS!

LIST 7 THINGS YOU ARE *grateful* FOR

Today I A.M. Grateful for

1. ____________________

Because: ____________________

____

2. ____________________

Because: ____________________

____

3. ____________________

Because: ____________________

____

4. ____________________

Because: ____________________

____

5. ____________________

Because: ____________________

____

6. ____________________

Because: ____________________

____

7. ____________________

Because: ____________________

____

Once you finish, go back and read everything and say to yourself or out loud: "Thank You God for this blessing" after each blessing. Having an attitude of gratitude will attract more to be grateful for in your life.

____ / ____ / ____

COUNT YOUR BLESSINGS!

LIST 7 THINGS YOU ARE *grateful* FOR

Today I A.M. Grateful for

1. ____________________

Because: ____________________

____

2. ____________________

Because: ____________________

____

3. ____________________

Because: ____________________

____

4. ____________________

Because: ____________________

____

5. ____________________

Because: ____________________

____

6. ____________________

Because: ____________________

____

7. ____________________

Because: ____________________

____

Once you finish, go back and read everything and say to yourself or out loud: "Thank You God for this blessing" after each blessing. Having an attitude of gratitude will attract more to be grateful for in your life.

____ /____ /____

COUNT YOUR BLESSINGS!

LIST 7 THINGS YOU ARE *grateful* FOR

Today I A.M. Grateful for

1. ______________________________

Because: ______________________________

____

2. ______________________________

Because: ______________________________

____

3. ______________________________

Because: ______________________________

____

4. ______________________________

Because: ______________________________

____

5. ______________________________

Because: ______________________________

____

6. ______________________________

Because: ______________________________

____

7. ______________________________

Because: ______________________________

____

Once you finish, go back and read everything and say to yourself or out loud: "Thank You God for this blessing" after each blessing. Having an attitude of gratitude will attract more to be grateful for in your life.

____ / ____ / ____

COUNT YOUR BLESSINGS!

LIST 7 THINGS YOU ARE *grateful* FOR

Today I A.M. Grateful for

1. ____________________

Because: ____________________

____

2. ____________________

Because: ____________________

____

3. ____________________

Because: ____________________

____

4. ____________________

Because: ____________________

____

5. ____________________

Because: ____________________

____

6. ____________________

Because: ____________________

____

7. ____________________

Because: ____________________

____

Once you finish, go back and read everything and say to yourself or out loud: "Thank You God for this blessing" after each blessing. Having an attitude of gratitude will attract more to be grateful for in your life.

Dream bigger, see greater,

have faith

and believe in all that
is possible for you.

____ / ____ / ____

COUNT YOUR BLESSINGS!

LIST 7 THINGS YOU ARE *grateful* FOR

Today I A.M. Grateful for

1. ______________________________

Because: ______________________________

____

2. ______________________________

Because: ______________________________

____

3. ______________________________

Because: ______________________________

____

4. ______________________________

Because: ______________________________

____

5. ______________________________

Because: ______________________________

____

6. ______________________________

Because: ______________________________

____

7. ______________________________

Because: ______________________________

____

Once you finish, go back and read everything and say to yourself or out loud: "Thank You God for this blessing" after each blessing. Having an attitude of gratitude will attract more to be grateful for in your life.

____ /____ /____

COUNT YOUR BLESSINGS!

LIST 7 THINGS YOU ARE *grateful* FOR

Today I A.M. Grateful for

1. ______________________________

Because: ______________________________

____

2. ______________________________

Because: ______________________________

____

3. ______________________________

Because: ______________________________

____

4. ______________________________

Because: ______________________________

____

5. ______________________________

Because: ______________________________

____

6. ______________________________

Because: ______________________________

____

7. ______________________________

Because: ______________________________

____

Once you finish, go back and read everything and say to yourself or out loud: "Thank You God for this blessing" after each blessing. Having an attitude of gratitude will attract more to be grateful for in your life.

____ / ____ / ____

COUNT YOUR BLESSINGS!

LIST 7 THINGS YOU ARE *grateful* FOR

Today I A.M. Grateful for

1. ____________________

Because: ____________________

____

2. ____________________

Because: ____________________

____

3. ____________________

Because: ____________________

____

4. ____________________

Because: ____________________

____

5. ____________________

Because: ____________________

____

6. ____________________

Because: ____________________

____

7. ____________________

Because: ____________________

____

Once you finish, go back and read everything and say to yourself or out loud: "Thank You God for this blessing" after each blessing. Having an attitude of gratitude will attract more to be grateful for in your life.

____ /____ /____

COUNT YOUR BLESSINGS!

LIST 7 THINGS YOU ARE *grateful* FOR

Today I A.M. Grateful for

1. ____________________
Because: ____________________
____

2. ____________________
Because: ____________________
____

3. ____________________
Because: ____________________
____

4. ____________________
Because: ____________________
____

5. ____________________
Because: ____________________
____

6. ____________________
Because: ____________________
____

7. ____________________
Because: ____________________
____

Once you finish, go back and read everything and say to yourself or out loud: "Thank You God for this blessing" after each blessing. Having an attitude of gratitude will attract more to be grateful for in your life.

____ / ____ / ____

COUNT YOUR BLESSINGS!

LIST 7 THINGS YOU ARE *grateful* FOR

Today I A.M. Grateful for

1. ______________________________

Because: ______________________________

____

2. ______________________________

Because: ______________________________

____

3. ______________________________

Because: ______________________________

____

4. ______________________________

Because: ______________________________

____

5. ______________________________

Because: ______________________________

____

6. ______________________________

Because: ______________________________

____

7. ______________________________

Because: ______________________________

____

Once you finish, go back and read everything and say to yourself or out loud: "Thank You God for this blessing" after each blessing. Having an attitude of gratitude will attract more to be grateful for in your life.

____ /____ /____

COUNT YOUR BLESSINGS!

LIST 7 THINGS YOU ARE *grateful* FOR

Today I A.M. Grateful for

1. ____________________

Because: ____________________

____

2. ____________________

Because: ____________________

____

3. ____________________

Because: ____________________

____

4. ____________________

Because: ____________________

____

5. ____________________

Because: ____________________

____

6. ____________________

Because: ____________________

____

7. ____________________

Because: ____________________

____

Once you finish, go back and read everything and say to yourself or out loud: "Thank You God for this blessing" after each blessing. Having an attitude of gratitude will attract more to be grateful for in your life.

____ / ____ / ____

COUNT YOUR BLESSINGS!

LIST 7 THINGS YOU ARE *grateful* FOR

Today I A.M. Grateful for

1. ______________________________

Because: ______________________________

____

2. ______________________________

Because: ______________________________

____

3. ______________________________

Because: ______________________________

____

4. ______________________________

Because: ______________________________

____

5. ______________________________

Because: ______________________________

____

6. ______________________________

Because: ______________________________

____

7. ______________________________

Because: ______________________________

____

Once you finish, go back and read everything and say to yourself or out loud: "Thank You God for this blessing" after each blessing. Having an attitude of gratitude will attract more to be grateful for in your life.

____ / ____ / ____

COUNT YOUR BLESSINGS!

LIST 7 THINGS YOU ARE *grateful* FOR

Today I A.M. Grateful for

1. ____________________
Because: ____________________
____

2. ____________________
Because: ____________________
____

3. ____________________
Because: ____________________
____

4. ____________________
Because: ____________________
____

5. ____________________
Because: ____________________
____

6. ____________________
Because: ____________________
____

7. ____________________
Because: ____________________
____

Once you finish, go back and read everything and say to yourself or out loud: "Thank You God for this blessing" after each blessing. Having an attitude of gratitude will attract more to be grateful for in your life.

____ / ____ / ____

COUNT YOUR BLESSINGS!

LIST 7 THINGS YOU ARE *grateful* FOR

Today I A.M. Grateful for

1. ____________________

Because: ____________________

2. ____________________

Because: ____________________

3. ____________________

Because: ____________________

4. ____________________

Because: ____________________

5. ____________________

Because: ____________________

6. ____________________

Because: ____________________

7. ____________________

Because: ____________________

Once you finish, go back and read everything and say to yourself or out loud: "Thank You God for this blessing" after each blessing. Having an attitude of gratitude will attract more to be grateful for in your life.

____ / ____ / ____

COUNT YOUR BLESSINGS!

LIST 7 THINGS YOU ARE *grateful* FOR

Today I A.M. Grateful for

1. ______________________

Because: ______________________

____

2. ______________________

Because: ______________________

____

3. ______________________

Because: ______________________

____

4. ______________________

Because: ______________________

____

5. ______________________

Because: ______________________

____

6. ______________________

Because: ______________________

____

7. ______________________

Because: ______________________

____

Once you finish, go back and read everything and say to yourself or out loud: "Thank You God for this blessing" after each blessing. Having an attitude of gratitude will attract more to be grateful for in your life.

____ / ____ / ____

COUNT YOUR BLESSINGS!

LIST 7 THINGS YOU ARE *grateful* FOR

Today I A.M. Grateful for

1. ____________________

Because: ____________________

2. ____________________

Because: ____________________

3. ____________________

Because: ____________________

4. ____________________

Because: ____________________

5. ____________________

Because: ____________________

6. ____________________

Because: ____________________

7. ____________________

Because: ____________________

Once you finish, go back and read everything and say to yourself or out loud: "Thank You God for this blessing" after each blessing. Having an attitude of gratitude will attract more to be grateful for in your life.

____ / ____ / ____

COUNT YOUR BLESSINGS!

LIST 7 THINGS YOU ARE *grateful* FOR

Today I A.M. Grateful for

1. ________________________________

Because: ________________________________

____

2. ________________________________

Because: ________________________________

____

3. ________________________________

Because: ________________________________

____

4. ________________________________

Because: ________________________________

____

5. ________________________________

Because: ________________________________

____

6. ________________________________

Because: ________________________________

____

7. ________________________________

Because: ________________________________

____

Once you finish, go back and read everything and say to yourself or out loud: "Thank You God for this blessing" after each blessing. Having an attitude of gratitude will attract more to be grateful for in your life.

____ / ____ / ____

COUNT YOUR BLESSINGS!

LIST 7 THINGS YOU ARE *grateful* FOR

Today I A.M. Grateful for

1. ____________________

Because: ____________________

____

2. ____________________

Because: ____________________

____

3. ____________________

Because: ____________________

____

4. ____________________

Because: ____________________

____

5. ____________________

Because: ____________________

____

6. ____________________

Because: ____________________

____

7. ____________________

Because: ____________________

____

Once you finish, go back and read everything and say to yourself or out loud: "Thank You God for this blessing" after each blessing. Having an attitude of gratitude will attract more to be grateful for in your life.

____ /____ /____

COUNT YOUR BLESSINGS!

LIST 7 THINGS YOU ARE *grateful* FOR

Today I A.M. Grateful for

1. ____________________

Because: ____________________

____

2. ____________________

Because: ____________________

____

3. ____________________

Because: ____________________

____

4. ____________________

Because: ____________________

____

5. ____________________

Because: ____________________

____

6. ____________________

Because: ____________________

____

7. ____________________

Because: ____________________

____

Once you finish, go back and read everything and say to yourself or out loud: "Thank You God for this blessing" after each blessing. Having an attitude of gratitude will attract more to be grateful for in your life.

____ / ____ / ____

COUNT YOUR BLESSINGS!

LIST 7 THINGS YOU ARE *grateful* FOR

Today I A.M. Grateful for

1. ____________________

Because: ____________________

____

2. ____________________

Because: ____________________

____

3. ____________________

Because: ____________________

____

4. ____________________

Because: ____________________

____

5. ____________________

Because: ____________________

____

6. ____________________

Because: ____________________

____

7. ____________________

Because: ____________________

____

Once you finish, go back and read everything and say to yourself or out loud: "Thank You God for this blessing" after each blessing. Having an attitude of gratitude will attract more to be grateful for in your life.

____ / ____ / ____

COUNT YOUR BLESSINGS!

LIST 7 THINGS YOU ARE *grateful* FOR

Today I A.M. Grateful for

1. ______________________________

Because: ______________________________

____

2. ______________________________

Because: ______________________________

____

3. ______________________________

Because: ______________________________

____

4. ______________________________

Because: ______________________________

____

5. ______________________________

Because: ______________________________

____

6. ______________________________

Because: ______________________________

____

7. ______________________________

Because: ______________________________

____

Once you finish, go back and read everything and say to yourself or out loud: "Thank You God for this blessing" after each blessing. Having an attitude of gratitude will attract more to be grateful for in your life.

____ / ____ / ____

COUNT YOUR BLESSINGS!

LIST 7 THINGS YOU ARE *grateful* FOR

Today I A.M. Grateful for

1. ____________________

Because: ____________________

____

2. ____________________

Because: ____________________

____

3. ____________________

Because: ____________________

____

4. ____________________

Because: ____________________

____

5. ____________________

Because: ____________________

____

6. ____________________

Because: ____________________

____

7. ____________________

Because: ____________________

____

Once you finish, go back and read everything and say to yourself or out loud: "Thank You God for this blessing" after each blessing. Having an attitude of gratitude will attract more to be grateful for in your life.

____ /____ /____

COUNT YOUR BLESSINGS!

LIST 7 THINGS YOU ARE *grateful* FOR

Today I A.M. Grateful for

1. ____________________

Because: ____________________

____

2. ____________________

Because: ____________________

____

3. ____________________

Because: ____________________

____

4. ____________________

Because: ____________________

____

5. ____________________

Because: ____________________

____

6. ____________________

Because: ____________________

____

7. ____________________

Because: ____________________

____

Once you finish, go back and read everything and say to yourself or out loud: "Thank You God for this blessing" after each blessing. Having an attitude of gratitude will attract more to be grateful for in your life.

____ /____ /____

COUNT YOUR BLESSINGS!

LIST 7 THINGS YOU ARE *grateful* FOR

Today I A.M. Grateful for

1. ____________________

Because: ____________________

____

2. ____________________

Because: ____________________

____

3. ____________________

Because: ____________________

____

4. ____________________

Because: ____________________

____

5. ____________________

Because: ____________________

____

6. ____________________

Because: ____________________

____

7. ____________________

Because: ____________________

____

Once you finish, go back and read everything and say to yourself or out loud: "Thank You God for this blessing" after each blessing. Having an attitude of gratitude will attract more to be grateful for in your life.

____ /____ /____

COUNT YOUR BLESSINGS!

LIST 7 THINGS YOU ARE *grateful* FOR

Today I A.M. Grateful for

1. ________________________________

Because: ________________________________

____

2. ________________________________

Because: ________________________________

____

3. ________________________________

Because: ________________________________

____

4. ________________________________

Because: ________________________________

____

5. ________________________________

Because: ________________________________

____

6. ________________________________

Because: ________________________________

____

7. ________________________________

Because: ________________________________

____

Once you finish, go back and read everything and say to yourself or out loud: "Thank You God for this blessing" after each blessing. Having an attitude of gratitude will attract more to be grateful for in your life.

____ / ____ / ____

COUNT YOUR BLESSINGS!

LIST 7 THINGS YOU ARE *grateful* FOR

Today I A.M. Grateful for

1. ______________________________

Because: ______________________________

____

2. ______________________________

Because: ______________________________

____

3. ______________________________

Because: ______________________________

____

4. ______________________________

Because: ______________________________

____

5. ______________________________

Because: ______________________________

____

6. ______________________________

Because: ______________________________

____

7. ______________________________

Because: ______________________________

____

Once you finish, go back and read everything and say to yourself or out loud: "Thank You God for this blessing" after each blessing. Having an attitude of gratitude will attract more to be grateful for in your life.

____ / ____ / ____

COUNT YOUR BLESSINGS!

LIST 7 THINGS YOU ARE *grateful* FOR

Today I A.M. Grateful for

1. ____________________

Because: ____________________

2. ____________________

Because: ____________________

3. ____________________

Because: ____________________

4. ____________________

Because: ____________________

5. ____________________

Because: ____________________

6. ____________________

Because: ____________________

7. ____________________

Because: ____________________

Once you finish, go back and read everything and say to yourself or out loud: "Thank You God for this blessing" after each blessing. Having an attitude of gratitude will attract more to be grateful for in your life.

____ /____ /____

COUNT YOUR BLESSINGS!

LIST 7 THINGS YOU ARE *grateful* FOR

Today I A.M. Grateful for

1. ______________________________

Because: ______________________________

____

2. ______________________________

Because: ______________________________

____

3. ______________________________

Because: ______________________________

____

4. ______________________________

Because: ______________________________

____

5. ______________________________

Because: ______________________________

____

6. ______________________________

Because: ______________________________

____

7. ______________________________

Because: ______________________________

____

Once you finish, go back and read everything and say to yourself or out loud: "Thank You God for this blessing" after each blessing. Having an attitude of gratitude will attract more to be grateful for in your life.

____ /____ /____

COUNT YOUR BLESSINGS!

LIST 7 THINGS YOU ARE *grateful* FOR

Today I A.M. Grateful for

1. ______________________________

Because: ______________________________

____

2. ______________________________

Because: ______________________________

____

3. ______________________________

Because: ______________________________

____

4. ______________________________

Because: ______________________________

____

5. ______________________________

Because: ______________________________

____

6. ______________________________

Because: ______________________________

____

7. ______________________________

Because: ______________________________

____

Once you finish, go back and read everything and say to yourself or out loud: "Thank You God for this blessing" after each blessing. Having an attitude of gratitude will attract more to be grateful for in your life.

____ / ____ / ____

COUNT YOUR BLESSINGS!

LIST 7 THINGS YOU ARE *grateful* FOR

Today I A.M. Grateful for

1. ______________________________

Because: ______________________________

____

2. ______________________________

Because: ______________________________

____

3. ______________________________

Because: ______________________________

____

4. ______________________________

Because: ______________________________

____

5. ______________________________

Because: ______________________________

____

6. ______________________________

Because: ______________________________

____

7. ______________________________

Because: ______________________________

____

Once you finish, go back and read everything and say to yourself or out loud: "Thank You God for this blessing" after each blessing. Having an attitude of gratitude will attract more to be grateful for in your life.

____ / ____ / ____

COUNT YOUR BLESSINGS!

LIST 7 THINGS YOU ARE *grateful* FOR

Today I A.M. Grateful for

1. ____________________

Because: ____________________

____

2. ____________________

Because: ____________________

____

3. ____________________

Because: ____________________

____

4. ____________________

Because: ____________________

____

5. ____________________

Because: ____________________

____

6. ____________________

Because: ____________________

____

7. ____________________

Because: ____________________

____

Once you finish, go back and read everything and say to yourself or out loud: "Thank You God for this blessing" after each blessing. Having an attitude of gratitude will attract more to be grateful for in your life.

____ / ____ / ____

COUNT YOUR BLESSINGS!

LIST 7 THINGS YOU ARE *grateful* FOR

Today I A.M. Grateful for

1. ______________________________

Because: ______________________________

____

2. ______________________________

Because: ______________________________

____

3. ______________________________

Because: ______________________________

____

4. ______________________________

Because: ______________________________

____

5. ______________________________

Because: ______________________________

____

6. ______________________________

Because: ______________________________

____

7. ______________________________

Because: ______________________________

____

Once you finish, go back and read everything and say to yourself or out loud: "Thank You God for this blessing" after each blessing. Having an attitude of gratitude will attract more to be grateful for in your life.

____ / ____ / ____

COUNT YOUR BLESSINGS!

LIST 7 THINGS YOU ARE *grateful* FOR

Today I A.M. Grateful for

1. ______________________________

Because: ______________________________

____

2. ______________________________

Because: ______________________________

____

3. ______________________________

Because: ______________________________

____

4. ______________________________

Because: ______________________________

____

5. ______________________________

Because: ______________________________

____

6. ______________________________

Because: ______________________________

____

7. ______________________________

Because: ______________________________

____

Once you finish, go back and read everything and say to yourself or out loud: "Thank You God for this blessing" after each blessing. Having an attitude of gratitude will attract more to be grateful for in your life.

____ / ____ / ____

COUNT YOUR BLESSINGS!

LIST 7 THINGS YOU ARE *grateful* FOR

Today I A.M. Grateful for

1. ______________________

Because: ______________________

____

2. ______________________

Because: ______________________

____

3. ______________________

Because: ______________________

____

4. ______________________

Because: ______________________

____

5. ______________________

Because: ______________________

____

6. ______________________

Because: ______________________

____

7. ______________________

Because: ______________________

____

Once you finish, go back and read everything and say to yourself or out loud: "Thank You God for this blessing" after each blessing. Having an attitude of gratitude will attract more to be grateful for in your life.

____ /____ /____

COUNT YOUR BLESSINGS!

LIST 7 THINGS YOU ARE *grateful* FOR

Today I A.M. Grateful for

1. ______________________________

Because: ______________________________

____

2. ______________________________

Because: ______________________________

____

3. ______________________________

Because: ______________________________

____

4. ______________________________

Because: ______________________________

____

5. ______________________________

Because: ______________________________

____

6. ______________________________

Because: ______________________________

____

7. ______________________________

Because: ______________________________

____

Once you finish, go back and read everything and say to yourself or out loud: "Thank You God for this blessing" after each blessing. Having an attitude of gratitude will attract more to be grateful for in your life.

_____ /_____ /_____

COUNT YOUR BLESSINGS!

LIST 7 THINGS YOU ARE *grateful* FOR

Today I A.M. Grateful for

1. ______________________________

Because: ______________________________

____

2. ______________________________

Because: ______________________________

____

3. ______________________________

Because: ______________________________

____

4. ______________________________

Because: ______________________________

____

5. ______________________________

Because: ______________________________

____

6. ______________________________

Because: ______________________________

____

7. ______________________________

Because: ______________________________

____

Once you finish, go back and read everything and say to yourself or out loud: "Thank You God for this blessing" after each blessing. Having an attitude of gratitude will attract more to be grateful for in your life.

____ /____ /____

COUNT YOUR BLESSINGS!

LIST 7 THINGS YOU ARE *grateful* FOR

Today I A.M. Grateful for

1. ________________________________

Because: ________________________________

____

2. ________________________________

Because: ________________________________

____

3. ________________________________

Because: ________________________________

____

4. ________________________________

Because: ________________________________

____

5. ________________________________

Because: ________________________________

____

6. ________________________________

Because: ________________________________

____

7. ________________________________

Because: ________________________________

____

Once you finish, go back and read everything and say to yourself or out loud: "Thank You God for this blessing" after each blessing. Having an attitude of gratitude will attract more to be grateful for in your life.

____ / ____ / ____

COUNT YOUR BLESSINGS!

LIST 7 THINGS YOU ARE *grateful* FOR

Today I A.M. Grateful for

1. ____

Because: ____

____

2. ____

Because: ____

____

3. ____

Because: ____

____

4. ____

Because: ____

____

5. ____

Because: ____

____

6. ____

Because: ____

____

7. ____

Because: ____

____

Once you finish, go back and read everything and say to yourself or out loud: "Thank You God for this blessing" after each blessing. Having an attitude of gratitude will attract more to be grateful for in your life.

___ / ___ / ___

COUNT YOUR BLESSINGS!

LIST 7 THINGS YOU ARE *grateful* FOR

Today I A.M. Grateful for

1. ______________________________

Because: ______________________________

____

2. ______________________________

Because: ______________________________

____

3. ______________________________

Because: ______________________________

____

4. ______________________________

Because: ______________________________

____

5. ______________________________

Because: ______________________________

____

6. ______________________________

Because: ______________________________

____

7. ______________________________

Because: ______________________________

____

Once you finish, go back and read everything and say to yourself or out loud: "Thank You God for this blessing" after each blessing. Having an attitude of gratitude will attract more to be grateful for in your life.

____ / ____ / ____

COUNT YOUR BLESSINGS!

LIST 7 THINGS YOU ARE *grateful* FOR

Today I A.M. Grateful for

1. ____________________

Because: ____________________

____

2. ____________________

Because: ____________________

____

3. ____________________

Because: ____________________

____

4. ____________________

Because: ____________________

____

5. ____________________

Because: ____________________

____

6. ____________________

Because: ____________________

____

7. ____________________

Because: ____________________

____

Once you finish, go back and read everything and say to yourself or out loud: "Thank You God for this blessing" after each blessing. Having an attitude of gratitude will attract more to be grateful for in your life.

Use the power of your mind
and words to

speak change,

everything you think and say can
happen!

_____ / _____ / _____

COUNT YOUR BLESSINGS!

LIST 7 THINGS YOU ARE *grateful* FOR

Today I A.M. Grateful for

1. ______________________________

Because: ______________________________

____

2. ______________________________

Because: ______________________________

____

3. ______________________________

Because: ______________________________

____

4. ______________________________

Because: ______________________________

____

5. ______________________________

Because: ______________________________

____

6. ______________________________

Because: ______________________________

____

7. ______________________________

Because: ______________________________

____

Once you finish, go back and read everything and say to yourself or out loud: "Thank You God for this blessing" after each blessing. Having an attitude of gratitude will attract more to be grateful for in your life.

____ /____ /____

COUNT YOUR BLESSINGS!

LIST 7 THINGS YOU ARE *grateful* FOR

Today I A.M. Grateful for

1. ________________________________

Because: ________________________________

____

2. ________________________________

Because: ________________________________

____

3. ________________________________

Because: ________________________________

____

4. ________________________________

Because: ________________________________

____

5. ________________________________

Because: ________________________________

____

6. ________________________________

Because: ________________________________

____

7. ________________________________

Because: ________________________________

____

Once you finish, go back and read everything and say to yourself or out loud: "Thank You God for this blessing" after each blessing. Having an attitude of gratitude will attract more to be grateful for in your life.

____ / ____ / ____

COUNT YOUR BLESSINGS!

LIST 7 THINGS YOU ARE *grateful* FOR

Today I A.M. Grateful for

1. ______________________________

Because: ______________________________

____

2. ______________________________

Because: ______________________________

____

3. ______________________________

Because: ______________________________

____

4. ______________________________

Because: ______________________________

____

5. ______________________________

Because: ______________________________

____

6. ______________________________

Because: ______________________________

____

7. ______________________________

Because: ______________________________

____

Once you finish, go back and read everything and say to yourself or out loud: "Thank You God for this blessing" after each blessing. Having an attitude of gratitude will attract more to be grateful for in your life.

____ / ____ / ____

COUNT YOUR BLESSINGS!

LIST 7 THINGS YOU ARE *grateful* FOR

Today I A.M. Grateful for

1. ________________________________

Because: ________________________________

____

2. ________________________________

Because: ________________________________

____

3. ________________________________

Because: ________________________________

____

4. ________________________________

Because: ________________________________

____

5. ________________________________

Because: ________________________________

____

6. ________________________________

Because: ________________________________

____

7. ________________________________

Because: ________________________________

____

Once you finish, go back and read everything and say to yourself or out loud: "Thank You God for this blessing" after each blessing. Having an attitude of gratitude will attract more to be grateful for in your life.

____ /____ /____

COUNT YOUR BLESSINGS!

LIST 7 THINGS YOU ARE *grateful* FOR

Today I A.M. Grateful for

1. ____________________

Because: ____________________

____

2. ____________________

Because: ____________________

____

3. ____________________

Because: ____________________

____

4. ____________________

Because: ____________________

____

5. ____________________

Because: ____________________

____

6. ____________________

Because: ____________________

____

7. ____________________

Because: ____________________

____

Once you finish, go back and read everything and say to yourself or out loud: "Thank You God for this blessing" after each blessing. Having an attitude of gratitude will attract more to be grateful for in your life.

____ / ____ / ____

COUNT YOUR BLESSINGS!

LIST 7 THINGS YOU ARE *grateful* FOR

Today I A.M. Grateful for

1. ____________________

Because: ____________________

2. ____________________

Because: ____________________

3. ____________________

Because: ____________________

4. ____________________

Because: ____________________

5. ____________________

Because: ____________________

6. ____________________

Because: ____________________

7. ____________________

Because: ____________________

Once you finish, go back and read everything and say to yourself or out loud: "Thank You God for this blessing" after each blessing. Having an attitude of gratitude will attract more to be grateful for in your life.

____ / ____ / ____

COUNT YOUR BLESSINGS!

LIST 7 THINGS YOU ARE *grateful* FOR

Today I A.M. Grateful for

1. ______________________________

Because: ______________________________

____

2. ______________________________

Because: ______________________________

____

3. ______________________________

Because: ______________________________

____

4. ______________________________

Because: ______________________________

____

5. ______________________________

Because: ______________________________

____

6. ______________________________

Because: ______________________________

____

7. ______________________________

Because: ______________________________

____

Once you finish, go back and read everything and say to yourself or out loud: "Thank You God for this blessing" after each blessing. Having an attitude of gratitude will attract more to be grateful for in your life.

_____ / _____ / _____

COUNT YOUR BLESSINGS!

LIST 7 THINGS YOU ARE *grateful* FOR

Today I A.M. Grateful for

1. ______________________________

Because: ______________________________

____

2. ______________________________

Because: ______________________________

____

3. ______________________________

Because: ______________________________

____

4. ______________________________

Because: ______________________________

____

5. ______________________________

Because: ______________________________

____

6. ______________________________

Because: ______________________________

____

7. ______________________________

Because: ______________________________

____

Once you finish, go back and read everything and say to yourself or out loud: "Thank You God for this blessing" after each blessing. Having an attitude of gratitude will attract more to be grateful for in your life.

____ / ____ / ____

COUNT YOUR BLESSINGS!

LIST 7 THINGS YOU ARE *grateful* FOR

Today I A.M. Grateful for

1. ______________________________

Because: ______________________________

____

2. ______________________________

Because: ______________________________

____

3. ______________________________

Because: ______________________________

____

4. ______________________________

Because: ______________________________

____

5. ______________________________

Because: ______________________________

____

6. ______________________________

Because: ______________________________

____

7. ______________________________

Because: ______________________________

____

Once you finish, go back and read everything and say to yourself or out loud: "Thank You God for this blessing" after each blessing. Having an attitude of gratitude will attract more to be grateful for in your life.

____ / ____ / ____

COUNT YOUR BLESSINGS!

LIST 7 THINGS YOU ARE *grateful* FOR

Today I A.M. Grateful for

1. ______________________________

Because: ______________________________

____

2. ______________________________

Because: ______________________________

____

3. ______________________________

Because: ______________________________

____

4. ______________________________

Because: ______________________________

____

5. ______________________________

Because: ______________________________

____

6. ______________________________

Because: ______________________________

____

7. ______________________________

Because: ______________________________

____

Once you finish, go back and read everything and say to yourself or out loud: "Thank You God for this blessing" after each blessing. Having an attitude of gratitude will attract more to be grateful for in your life.

____ / ____ / ____

COUNT YOUR BLESSINGS!

LIST 7 THINGS YOU ARE *grateful* FOR

Today I A.M. Grateful for

1. ____________________

Because: ____________________

2. ____________________

Because: ____________________

3. ____________________

Because: ____________________

4. ____________________

Because: ____________________

5. ____________________

Because: ____________________

6. ____________________

Because: ____________________

7. ____________________

Because: ____________________

Once you finish, go back and read everything and say to yourself or out loud: "Thank You God for this blessing" after each blessing. Having an attitude of gratitude will attract more to be grateful for in your life.

____ /____ /____

COUNT YOUR BLESSINGS!

LIST 7 THINGS YOU ARE *grateful* FOR

Today I A.M. Grateful for

1. ______________________________

Because: ______________________________

____

2. ______________________________

Because: ______________________________

____

3. ______________________________

Because: ______________________________

____

4. ______________________________

Because: ______________________________

____

5. ______________________________

Because: ______________________________

____

6. ______________________________

Because: ______________________________

____

7. ______________________________

Because: ______________________________

____

Once you finish, go back and read everything and say to yourself or out loud: "Thank You God for this blessing" after each blessing. Having an attitude of gratitude will attract more to be grateful for in your life.

____ /____ /____

COUNT YOUR BLESSINGS!

LIST 7 THINGS YOU ARE *grateful* FOR

Today I A.M. Grateful for

1. ______________________________

Because: ______________________________

____

2. ______________________________

Because: ______________________________

____

3. ______________________________

Because: ______________________________

____

4. ______________________________

Because: ______________________________

____

5. ______________________________

Because: ______________________________

____

6. ______________________________

Because: ______________________________

____

7. ______________________________

Because: ______________________________

____

Once you finish, go back and read everything and say to yourself or out loud: "Thank You God for this blessing" after each blessing. Having an attitude of gratitude will attract more to be grateful for in your life.

____ /____ /____

COUNT YOUR BLESSINGS!

LIST 7 THINGS YOU ARE *grateful* FOR

Today I A.M. Grateful for

1. ____________________

Because: ____________________

____

2. ____________________

Because: ____________________

____

3. ____________________

Because: ____________________

____

4. ____________________

Because: ____________________

____

5. ____________________

Because: ____________________

____

6. ____________________

Because: ____________________

____

7. ____________________

Because: ____________________

____

Once you finish, go back and read everything and say to yourself or out loud: "Thank You God for this blessing" after each blessing. Having an attitude of gratitude will attract more to be grateful for in your life.

____ / ____ / ____

COUNT YOUR BLESSINGS!

LIST 7 THINGS YOU ARE *grateful* FOR

Today I A.M. Grateful for

1. ____________________

Because: ____________________

____

2. ____________________

Because: ____________________

____

3. ____________________

Because: ____________________

____

4. ____________________

Because: ____________________

____

5. ____________________

Because: ____________________

____

6. ____________________

Because: ____________________

____

7. ____________________

Because: ____________________

____

Once you finish, go back and read everything and say to yourself or out loud: "Thank You God for this blessing" after each blessing. Having an attitude of gratitude will attract more to be grateful for in your life.

____ /____ /____

COUNT YOUR BLESSINGS!

LIST 7 THINGS YOU ARE *grateful* FOR

Today I A.M. Grateful for

1. ______________________________

Because: ______________________________

____

2. ______________________________

Because: ______________________________

____

3. ______________________________

Because: ______________________________

____

4. ______________________________

Because: ______________________________

____

5. ______________________________

Because: ______________________________

____

6. ______________________________

Because: ______________________________

____

7. ______________________________

Because: ______________________________

____

Once you finish, go back and read everything and say to yourself or out loud: "Thank You God for this blessing" after each blessing. Having an attitude of gratitude will attract more to be grateful for in your life.

_____ / _____ / _____

COUNT YOUR BLESSINGS!

LIST 7 THINGS YOU ARE *grateful* FOR

Today I A.M. Grateful for

1. ____________________
Because: ____________________

2. ____________________
Because: ____________________

3. ____________________
Because: ____________________

4. ____________________
Because: ____________________

5. ____________________
Because: ____________________

6. ____________________
Because: ____________________

7. ____________________
Because: ____________________

Once you finish, go back and read everything and say to yourself or out loud: "Thank You God for this blessing" after each blessing. Having an attitude of gratitude will attract more to be grateful for in your life.

____ /____ /____

COUNT YOUR BLESSINGS!

LIST 7 THINGS YOU ARE *grateful* FOR

Today I A.M. Grateful for

1. ______________________________

Because: ______________________________

____

2. ______________________________

Because: ______________________________

____

3. ______________________________

Because: ______________________________

____

4. ______________________________

Because: ______________________________

____

5. ______________________________

Because: ______________________________

____

6. ______________________________

Because: ______________________________

____

7. ______________________________

Because: ______________________________

____

Once you finish, go back and read everything and say to yourself or out loud: "Thank You God for this blessing" after each blessing. Having an attitude of gratitude will attract more to be grateful for in your life.

____ / ____ / ____

COUNT YOUR BLESSINGS!

LIST 7 THINGS YOU ARE *grateful* FOR

Today I A.M. Grateful for

1. ______________________

Because: ______________________

____

2. ______________________

Because: ______________________

____

3. ______________________

Because: ______________________

____

4. ______________________

Because: ______________________

____

5. ______________________

Because: ______________________

____

6. ______________________

Because: ______________________

____

7. ______________________

Because: ______________________

____

Once you finish, go back and read everything and say to yourself or out loud: "Thank You God for this blessing" after each blessing. Having an attitude of gratitude will attract more to be grateful for in your life.

____ /____ /____

COUNT YOUR BLESSINGS!

LIST 7 THINGS YOU ARE *grateful* FOR

Today I A.M. Grateful for

1. ______________________________

Because: ______________________________

____

2. ______________________________

Because: ______________________________

____

3. ______________________________

Because: ______________________________

____

4. ______________________________

Because: ______________________________

____

5. ______________________________

Because: ______________________________

____

6. ______________________________

Because: ______________________________

____

7. ______________________________

Because: ______________________________

____

Once you finish, go back and read everything and say to yourself or out loud: "Thank You God for this blessing" after each blessing. Having an attitude of gratitude will attract more to be grateful for in your life.

____ / ____ / ____

COUNT YOUR BLESSINGS!

LIST 7 THINGS YOU ARE *grateful* FOR

Today I A.M. Grateful for

1. ____________________

Because: ____________________

____

2. ____________________

Because: ____________________

____

3. ____________________

Because: ____________________

____

4. ____________________

Because: ____________________

____

5. ____________________

Because: ____________________

____

6. ____________________

Because: ____________________

____

7. ____________________

Because: ____________________

____

Once you finish, go back and read everything and say to yourself or out loud: "Thank You God for this blessing" after each blessing. Having an attitude of gratitude will attract more to be grateful for in your life.

____ /____ /____

COUNT YOUR BLESSINGS!

LIST 7 THINGS YOU ARE *grateful* FOR

Today I A.M. Grateful for

1. ________________________________

Because: ________________________________

____

2. ________________________________

Because: ________________________________

____

3. ________________________________

Because: ________________________________

____

4. ________________________________

Because: ________________________________

____

5. ________________________________

Because: ________________________________

____

6. ________________________________

Because: ________________________________

____

7. ________________________________

Because: ________________________________

____

Once you finish, go back and read everything and say to yourself or out loud: "Thank You God for this blessing" after each blessing. Having an attitude of gratitude will attract more to be grateful for in your life.

____ / ____ / ____

COUNT YOUR BLESSINGS!

LIST 7 THINGS YOU ARE *grateful* FOR

Today I A.M. Grateful for

1. ______________________________

Because: ______________________________

____

2. ______________________________

Because: ______________________________

____

3. ______________________________

Because: ______________________________

____

4. ______________________________

Because: ______________________________

____

5. ______________________________

Because: ______________________________

____

6. ______________________________

Because: ______________________________

____

7. ______________________________

Because: ______________________________

____

Once you finish, go back and read everything and say to yourself or out loud: "Thank You God for this blessing" after each blessing. Having an attitude of gratitude will attract more to be grateful for in your life.

____ / ____ / ____

COUNT YOUR BLESSINGS!

LIST 7 THINGS YOU ARE *grateful* FOR

Today I A.M. Grateful for

1. ______________________________

Because: ______________________________

____

2. ______________________________

Because: ______________________________

____

3. ______________________________

Because: ______________________________

____

4. ______________________________

Because: ______________________________

____

5. ______________________________

Because: ______________________________

____

6. ______________________________

Because: ______________________________

____

7. ______________________________

Because: ______________________________

____

Once you finish, go back and read everything and say to yourself or out loud: "Thank You God for this blessing" after each blessing. Having an attitude of gratitude will attract more to be grateful for in your life.

____ /____ /____

COUNT YOUR BLESSINGS!

LIST 7 THINGS YOU ARE *grateful* FOR

Today I A.M. Grateful for

1. ____________________

Because: ____________________

____

2. ____________________

Because: ____________________

____

3. ____________________

Because: ____________________

____

4. ____________________

Because: ____________________

____

5. ____________________

Because: ____________________

____

6. ____________________

Because: ____________________

____

7. ____________________

Because: ____________________

____

Once you finish, go back and read everything and say to yourself or out loud: "Thank You God for this blessing" after each blessing. Having an attitude of gratitude will attract more to be grateful for in your life.

____ / ____ / ____

COUNT YOUR BLESSINGS!

LIST 7 THINGS YOU ARE *grateful* FOR

Today I A.M. Grateful for

1. ______________________________

Because: ______________________________

____

2. ______________________________

Because: ______________________________

____

3. ______________________________

Because: ______________________________

____

4. ______________________________

Because: ______________________________

____

5. ______________________________

Because: ______________________________

____

6. ______________________________

Because: ______________________________

____

7. ______________________________

Because: ______________________________

____

Once you finish, go back and read everything and say to yourself or out loud: "Thank You God for this blessing" after each blessing. Having an attitude of gratitude will attract more to be grateful for in your life.

____ / ____ / ____

COUNT YOUR BLESSINGS!

LIST 7 THINGS YOU ARE *grateful* FOR

Today I A.M. Grateful for

1. ____________________

Because: ____________________

____

2. ____________________

Because: ____________________

____

3. ____________________

Because: ____________________

____

4. ____________________

Because: ____________________

____

5. ____________________

Because: ____________________

____

6. ____________________

Because: ____________________

____

7. ____________________

Because: ____________________

____

Once you finish, go back and read everything and say to yourself or out loud: "Thank You God for this blessing" after each blessing. Having an attitude of gratitude will attract more to be grateful for in your life.

____ /____ /____

COUNT YOUR BLESSINGS!

LIST 7 THINGS YOU ARE *grateful* FOR

Today I A.M. Grateful for

1. ______________________________

Because: ______________________________

____

2. ______________________________

Because: ______________________________

____

3. ______________________________

Because: ______________________________

____

4. ______________________________

Because: ______________________________

____

5. ______________________________

Because: ______________________________

____

6. ______________________________

Because: ______________________________

____

7. ______________________________

Because: ______________________________

____

Once you finish, go back and read everything and say to yourself or out loud: "Thank You God for this blessing" after each blessing. Having an attitude of gratitude will attract more to be grateful for in your life.

____ / ____ / ____

COUNT YOUR BLESSINGS!

LIST 7 THINGS YOU ARE *grateful* FOR

Today I A.M. Grateful for

1. ____________________
Because: ____________________
____

2. ____________________
Because: ____________________
____

3. ____________________
Because: ____________________
____

4. ____________________
Because: ____________________
____

5. ____________________
Because: ____________________
____

6. ____________________
Because: ____________________
____

7. ____________________
Because: ____________________
____

Once you finish, go back and read everything and say to yourself or out loud: "Thank You God for this blessing" after each blessing. Having an attitude of gratitude will attract more to be grateful for in your life.

____ / ____ / ____

COUNT YOUR BLESSINGS!

LIST 7 THINGS YOU ARE *grateful* FOR

Today I A.M. Grateful for

1. ____________________

Because: ____________________

2. ____________________

Because: ____________________

3. ____________________

Because: ____________________

4. ____________________

Because: ____________________

5. ____________________

Because: ____________________

6. ____________________

Because: ____________________

7. ____________________

Because: ____________________

Once you finish, go back and read everything and say to yourself or out loud: "Thank You God for this blessing" after each blessing. Having an attitude of gratitude will attract more to be grateful for in your life.

____ /____ /____

COUNT YOUR BLESSINGS!

LIST 7 THINGS YOU ARE *grateful* FOR

Today I A.M. Grateful for

1. ____________________

Because: ____________________

____

2. ____________________

Because: ____________________

____

3. ____________________

Because: ____________________

____

4. ____________________

Because: ____________________

____

5. ____________________

Because: ____________________

____

6. ____________________

Because: ____________________

____

7. ____________________

Because: ____________________

____

Once you finish, go back and read everything and say to yourself or out loud: "Thank You God for this blessing" after each blessing. Having an attitude of gratitude will attract more to be grateful for in your life.

____ /____ /____

COUNT YOUR BLESSINGS!

LIST 7 THINGS YOU ARE *grateful* FOR

Today I A.M. Grateful for

1. ______________________________

Because: ______________________________

____

2. ______________________________

Because: ______________________________

____

3. ______________________________

Because: ______________________________

____

4. ______________________________

Because: ______________________________

____

5. ______________________________

Because: ______________________________

____

6. ______________________________

Because: ______________________________

____

7. ______________________________

Because: ______________________________

____

Once you finish, go back and read everything and say to yourself or out loud: "Thank You God for this blessing" after each blessing. Having an attitude of gratitude will attract more to be grateful for in your life.

____ / ____ / ____

COUNT YOUR BLESSINGS!

LIST 7 THINGS YOU ARE *grateful* FOR

Today I A.M. Grateful for

1. ____________________

Because: ____________________

2. ____________________

Because: ____________________

3. ____________________

Because: ____________________

4. ____________________

Because: ____________________

5. ____________________

Because: ____________________

6. ____________________

Because: ____________________

7. ____________________

Because: ____________________

Once you finish, go back and read everything and say to yourself or out loud: "Thank You God for this blessing" after each blessing. Having an attitude of gratitude will attract more to be grateful for in your life.

____ / ____ / ____

COUNT YOUR BLESSINGS!

LIST 7 THINGS YOU ARE *grateful* FOR

Today I A.M. Grateful for

1. ______________________________

Because: ______________________________

____

2. ______________________________

Because: ______________________________

____

3. ______________________________

Because: ______________________________

____

4. ______________________________

Because: ______________________________

____

5. ______________________________

Because: ______________________________

____

6. ______________________________

Because: ______________________________

____

7. ______________________________

Because: ______________________________

____

Once you finish, go back and read everything and say to yourself or out loud: "Thank You God for this blessing" after each blessing. Having an attitude of gratitude will attract more to be grateful for in your life.

____ / ____ / ____

COUNT YOUR BLESSINGS!

LIST 7 THINGS YOU ARE *grateful* FOR

Today I A.M. Grateful for

1. ____________________

Because: ____________________

____

2. ____________________

Because: ____________________

____

3. ____________________

Because: ____________________

____

4. ____________________

Because: ____________________

____

5. ____________________

Because: ____________________

____

6. ____________________

Because: ____________________

____

7. ____________________

Because: ____________________

____

Once you finish, go back and read everything and say to yourself or out loud: "Thank You God for this blessing" after each blessing. Having an attitude of gratitude will attract more to be grateful for in your life.

God didn't bring you this far for nothing. Don't get discouraged, stay positive, stay focused, and

keep going!

____ / ____ / ____

COUNT YOUR BLESSINGS!

LIST 7 THINGS YOU ARE *grateful* FOR

Today I A.M. Grateful for

1. ____________________
Because: ____________________
____

2. ____________________
Because: ____________________
____

3. ____________________
Because: ____________________
____

4. ____________________
Because: ____________________
____

5. ____________________
Because: ____________________
____

6. ____________________
Because: ____________________
____

7. ____________________
Because: ____________________
____

Once you finish, go back and read everything and say to yourself or out loud: "Thank You God for this blessing" after each blessing. Having an attitude of gratitude will attract more to be grateful for in your life.

____ /____ /____

COUNT YOUR BLESSINGS!

LIST 7 THINGS YOU ARE *grateful* FOR

Today I A.M. Grateful for

1. ______________________________

Because: ______________________________

____

2. ______________________________

Because: ______________________________

____

3. ______________________________

Because: ______________________________

____

4. ______________________________

Because: ______________________________

____

5. ______________________________

Because: ______________________________

____

6. ______________________________

Because: ______________________________

____

7. ______________________________

Because: ______________________________

____

Once you finish, go back and read everything and say to yourself or out loud: "Thank You God for this blessing" after each blessing. Having an attitude of gratitude will attract more to be grateful for in your life.

____ / ____ / ____

COUNT YOUR BLESSINGS!

LIST 7 THINGS YOU ARE *grateful* FOR

Today I A.M. Grateful for

1. ______________________________

Because: ______________________________

____

2. ______________________________

Because: ______________________________

____

3. ______________________________

Because: ______________________________

____

4. ______________________________

Because: ______________________________

____

5. ______________________________

Because: ______________________________

____

6. ______________________________

Because: ______________________________

____

7. ______________________________

Because: ______________________________

____

Once you finish, go back and read everything and say to yourself or out loud: "Thank You God for this blessing" after each blessing. Having an attitude of gratitude will attract more to be grateful for in your life.

____ / ____ / ____

COUNT YOUR BLESSINGS!

LIST 7 THINGS YOU ARE *grateful* FOR

Today I A.M. Grateful for

1. ____________________

Because: ____________________

2. ____________________

Because: ____________________

3. ____________________

Because: ____________________

4. ____________________

Because: ____________________

5. ____________________

Because: ____________________

6. ____________________

Because: ____________________

7. ____________________

Because: ____________________

Once you finish, go back and read everything and say to yourself or out loud: "Thank You God for this blessing" after each blessing. Having an attitude of gratitude will attract more to be grateful for in your life.

____ / ____ / ____

COUNT YOUR BLESSINGS!

LIST 7 THINGS YOU ARE *grateful* FOR

Today I A.M. Grateful for

1. ______________________________

Because: ______________________________

____

2. ______________________________

Because: ______________________________

____

3. ______________________________

Because: ______________________________

____

4. ______________________________

Because: ______________________________

____

5. ______________________________

Because: ______________________________

____

6. ______________________________

Because: ______________________________

____

7. ______________________________

Because: ______________________________

____

Once you finish, go back and read everything and say to yourself or out loud: "Thank You God for this blessing" after each blessing. Having an attitude of gratitude will attract more to be grateful for in your life.

____ /____ /____

COUNT YOUR BLESSINGS!

LIST 7 THINGS YOU ARE *grateful* FOR

Today I A.M. Grateful for

1. ____________________

Because: ____________________

____

2. ____________________

Because: ____________________

____

3. ____________________

Because: ____________________

____

4. ____________________

Because: ____________________

____

5. ____________________

Because: ____________________

____

6. ____________________

Because: ____________________

____

7. ____________________

Because: ____________________

____

Once you finish, go back and read everything and say to yourself or out loud: "Thank You God for this blessing" after each blessing. Having an attitude of gratitude will attract more to be grateful for in your life.

____ / ____ / ____

COUNT YOUR BLESSINGS!

LIST 7 THINGS YOU ARE *grateful* FOR

Today I A.M. Grateful for

1. ____________________

Because: ____________________

____

2. ____________________

Because: ____________________

____

3. ____________________

Because: ____________________

____

4. ____________________

Because: ____________________

____

5. ____________________

Because: ____________________

____

6. ____________________

Because: ____________________

____

7. ____________________

Because: ____________________

____

Once you finish, go back and read everything and say to yourself or out loud: "Thank You God for this blessing" after each blessing. Having an attitude of gratitude will attract more to be grateful for in your life.

____ /____ /____

COUNT YOUR BLESSINGS!

LIST 7 THINGS YOU ARE *grateful* FOR

Today I A.M. Grateful for

1. ______________________________

Because: ______________________________

____

2. ______________________________

Because: ______________________________

____

3. ______________________________

Because: ______________________________

____

4. ______________________________

Because: ______________________________

____

5. ______________________________

Because: ______________________________

____

6. ______________________________

Because: ______________________________

____

7. ______________________________

Because: ______________________________

____

Once you finish, go back and read everything and say to yourself or out loud: "Thank You God for this blessing" after each blessing. Having an attitude of gratitude will attract more to be grateful for in your life.

____ /____ /____

COUNT YOUR BLESSINGS!

LIST 7 THINGS YOU ARE *grateful* FOR

Today I A.M. Grateful for

1. ____________________

Because: ____________________

____

2. ____________________

Because: ____________________

____

3. ____________________

Because: ____________________

____

4. ____________________

Because: ____________________

____

5. ____________________

Because: ____________________

____

6. ____________________

Because: ____________________

____

7. ____________________

Because: ____________________

____

Once you finish, go back and read everything and say to yourself or out loud: "Thank You God for this blessing" after each blessing. Having an attitude of gratitude will attract more to be grateful for in your life.

____ /____ /____

COUNT YOUR BLESSINGS!

LIST 7 THINGS YOU ARE *grateful* FOR

Today I A.M. Grateful for

1. ______________________________

Because: ______________________________

____

2. ______________________________

Because: ______________________________

____

3. ______________________________

Because: ______________________________

____

4. ______________________________

Because: ______________________________

____

5. ______________________________

Because: ______________________________

____

6. ______________________________

Because: ______________________________

____

7. ______________________________

Because: ______________________________

____

Once you finish, go back and read everything and say to yourself or out loud: "Thank You God for this blessing" after each blessing. Having an attitude of gratitude will attract more to be grateful for in your life.

____ /____ /____

COUNT YOUR BLESSINGS!

LIST 7 THINGS YOU ARE *grateful* FOR

Today I A.M. Grateful for

1. ____________________

Because: ____________________

____

2. ____________________

Because: ____________________

____

3. ____________________

Because: ____________________

____

4. ____________________

Because: ____________________

____

5. ____________________

Because: ____________________

____

6. ____________________

Because: ____________________

____

7. ____________________

Because: ____________________

____

Once you finish, go back and read everything and say to yourself or out loud: "Thank You God for this blessing" after each blessing. Having an attitude of gratitude will attract more to be grateful for in your life.

____ /____ /____

COUNT YOUR BLESSINGS!

LIST 7 THINGS YOU ARE *grateful* FOR

Today I A.M. Grateful for

1. ____________________

Because: ____________________

____

2. ____________________

Because: ____________________

____

3. ____________________

Because: ____________________

____

4. ____________________

Because: ____________________

____

5. ____________________

Because: ____________________

____

6. ____________________

Because: ____________________

____

7. ____________________

Because: ____________________

____

Once you finish, go back and read everything and say to yourself or out loud: "Thank You God for this blessing" after each blessing. Having an attitude of gratitude will attract more to be grateful for in your life.

____ / ____ / ____

COUNT YOUR BLESSINGS!

LIST 7 THINGS YOU ARE *grateful* FOR

Today I A.M. Grateful for

1. ______________________________

Because: ______________________________

____

2. ______________________________

Because: ______________________________

____

3. ______________________________

Because: ______________________________

____

4. ______________________________

Because: ______________________________

____

5. ______________________________

Because: ______________________________

____

6. ______________________________

Because: ______________________________

____

7. ______________________________

Because: ______________________________

____

Once you finish, go back and read everything and say to yourself or out loud: "Thank You God for this blessing" after each blessing. Having an attitude of gratitude will attract more to be grateful for in your life.

____ /____ /____

COUNT YOUR BLESSINGS!

LIST 7 THINGS YOU ARE *grateful* FOR

Today I A.M. Grateful for

1. ____________________

Because: ____________________

____

2. ____________________

Because: ____________________

____

3. ____________________

Because: ____________________

____

4. ____________________

Because: ____________________

____

5. ____________________

Because: ____________________

____

6. ____________________

Because: ____________________

____

7. ____________________

Because: ____________________

____

Once you finish, go back and read everything and say to yourself or out loud: "Thank You God for this blessing" after each blessing. Having an attitude of gratitude will attract more to be grateful for in your life.

____ /____ /____

COUNT YOUR BLESSINGS!

LIST 7 THINGS YOU ARE *grateful* FOR

Today I A.M. Grateful for

1. ____________________

Because: ____________________

____

2. ____________________

Because: ____________________

____

3. ____________________

Because: ____________________

____

4. ____________________

Because: ____________________

____

5. ____________________

Because: ____________________

____

6. ____________________

Because: ____________________

____

7. ____________________

Because: ____________________

____

Once you finish, go back and read everything and say to yourself or out loud: "Thank You God for this blessing" after each blessing. Having an attitude of gratitude will attract more to be grateful for in your life.

____ / ____ / ____

COUNT YOUR BLESSINGS!

LIST 7 THINGS YOU ARE *grateful* FOR

Today I A.M. Grateful for

1. ____________________

Because: ____________________

2. ____________________

Because: ____________________

3. ____________________

Because: ____________________

4. ____________________

Because: ____________________

5. ____________________

Because: ____________________

6. ____________________

Because: ____________________

7. ____________________

Because: ____________________

Once you finish, go back and read everything and say to yourself or out loud: "Thank You God for this blessing" after each blessing. Having an attitude of gratitude will attract more to be grateful for in your life.

____ / ____ / ____

COUNT YOUR BLESSINGS!

LIST 7 THINGS YOU ARE *grateful* FOR

Today I A.M. Grateful for

1. ______________________________

Because: ______________________________

____

2. ______________________________

Because: ______________________________

____

3. ______________________________

Because: ______________________________

____

4. ______________________________

Because: ______________________________

____

5. ______________________________

Because: ______________________________

____

6. ______________________________

Because: ______________________________

____

7. ______________________________

Because: ______________________________

____

Once you finish, go back and read everything and say to yourself or out loud: "Thank You God for this blessing" after each blessing. Having an attitude of gratitude will attract more to be grateful for in your life.

____ /____ /____

COUNT YOUR BLESSINGS!

LIST 7 THINGS YOU ARE *grateful* FOR

Today I A.M. Grateful for

1. ____________________

Because: ____________________

____

2. ____________________

Because: ____________________

____

3. ____________________

Because: ____________________

____

4. ____________________

Because: ____________________

____

5. ____________________

Because: ____________________

____

6. ____________________

Because: ____________________

____

7. ____________________

Because: ____________________

____

Once you finish, go back and read everything and say to yourself or out loud: "Thank You God for this blessing" after each blessing. Having an attitude of gratitude will attract more to be grateful for in your life.

____ / ____ / ____

COUNT YOUR BLESSINGS!

LIST 7 THINGS YOU ARE *grateful* FOR

Today I A.M. Grateful for

1. ______________________________

Because: ______________________________

____

2. ______________________________

Because: ______________________________

____

3. ______________________________

Because: ______________________________

____

4. ______________________________

Because: ______________________________

____

5. ______________________________

Because: ______________________________

____

6. ______________________________

Because: ______________________________

____

7. ______________________________

Because: ______________________________

____

Once you finish, go back and read everything and say to yourself or out loud: "Thank You God for this blessing" after each blessing. Having an attitude of gratitude will attract more to be grateful for in your life.

____ /____ /____

COUNT YOUR BLESSINGS!

LIST 7 THINGS YOU ARE *grateful* FOR

Today I A.M. Grateful for

1. ______________________________

Because: ______________________________

____

2. ______________________________

Because: ______________________________

____

3. ______________________________

Because: ______________________________

____

4. ______________________________

Because: ______________________________

____

5. ______________________________

Because: ______________________________

____

6. ______________________________

Because: ______________________________

____

7. ______________________________

Because: ______________________________

____

Once you finish, go back and read everything and say to yourself or out loud: "Thank You God for this blessing" after each blessing. Having an attitude of gratitude will attract more to be grateful for in your life.

____ /____ /____

COUNT YOUR BLESSINGS!

LIST 7 THINGS YOU ARE *grateful* FOR

Today I A.M. Grateful for

1. ______________________________

Because: ______________________________

____

2. ______________________________

Because: ______________________________

____

3. ______________________________

Because: ______________________________

____

4. ______________________________

Because: ______________________________

____

5. ______________________________

Because: ______________________________

____

6. ______________________________

Because: ______________________________

____

7. ______________________________

Because: ______________________________

____

Once you finish, go back and read everything and say to yourself or out loud: "Thank You God for this blessing" after each blessing. Having an attitude of gratitude will attract more to be grateful for in your life.

____ / ____ / ____

COUNT YOUR BLESSINGS!

LIST 7 THINGS YOU ARE *grateful* FOR

Today I A.M. Grateful for

1. ________________________________

Because: ________________________________

2. ________________________________

Because: ________________________________

3. ________________________________

Because: ________________________________

4. ________________________________

Because: ________________________________

5. ________________________________

Because: ________________________________

6. ________________________________

Because: ________________________________

7. ________________________________

Because: ________________________________

Once you finish, go back and read everything and say to yourself or out loud: "Thank You God for this blessing" after each blessing. Having an attitude of gratitude will attract more to be grateful for in your life.

____ /____ /____

COUNT YOUR BLESSINGS!

LIST 7 THINGS YOU ARE *grateful* FOR

Today I A.M. Grateful for

1. ______________________________

Because: ______________________________

____

2. ______________________________

Because: ______________________________

____

3. ______________________________

Because: ______________________________

____

4. ______________________________

Because: ______________________________

____

5. ______________________________

Because: ______________________________

____

6. ______________________________

Because: ______________________________

____

7. ______________________________

Because: ______________________________

____

Once you finish, go back and read everything and say to yourself or out loud: "Thank You God for this blessing" after each blessing. Having an attitude of gratitude will attract more to be grateful for in your life.

____ / ____ / ____

COUNT YOUR BLESSINGS!

LIST 7 THINGS YOU ARE *grateful* FOR

Today I A.M. Grateful for

1. ____________________

Because: ____________________

____

2. ____________________

Because: ____________________

____

3. ____________________

Because: ____________________

____

4. ____________________

Because: ____________________

____

5. ____________________

Because: ____________________

____

6. ____________________

Because: ____________________

____

7. ____________________

Because: ____________________

____

Once you finish, go back and read everything and say to yourself or out loud: "Thank You God for this blessing" after each blessing. Having an attitude of gratitude will attract more to be grateful for in your life.

____ /____ /____

COUNT YOUR BLESSINGS!

LIST 7 THINGS YOU ARE *grateful* FOR

Today I A.M. Grateful for

1. ____________________

Because: ____________________

____

2. ____________________

Because: ____________________

____

3. ____________________

Because: ____________________

____

4. ____________________

Because: ____________________

____

5. ____________________

Because: ____________________

____

6. ____________________

Because: ____________________

____

7. ____________________

Because: ____________________

____

Once you finish, go back and read everything and say to yourself or out loud: "Thank You God for this blessing" after each blessing. Having an attitude of gratitude will attract more to be grateful for in your life.

____ / ____ / ____

COUNT YOUR BLESSINGS!

LIST 7 THINGS YOU ARE *grateful* FOR

Today I A.M. Grateful for

1. ____

Because: ____

2. ____

Because: ____

3. ____

Because: ____

4. ____

Because: ____

5. ____

Because: ____

6. ____

Because: ____

7. ____

Because: ____

Once you finish, go back and read everything and say to yourself or out loud: "Thank You God for this blessing" after each blessing. Having an attitude of gratitude will attract more to be grateful for in your life.

____ / ____ / ____

COUNT YOUR BLESSINGS!

LIST 7 THINGS YOU ARE *grateful* FOR

Today I A.M. Grateful for

1. ______________________________

Because: ______________________________

____

2. ______________________________

Because: ______________________________

____

3. ______________________________

Because: ______________________________

____

4. ______________________________

Because: ______________________________

____

5. ______________________________

Because: ______________________________

____

6. ______________________________

Because: ______________________________

____

7. ______________________________

Because: ______________________________

____

Once you finish, go back and read everything and say to yourself or out loud: "Thank You God for this blessing" after each blessing. Having an attitude of gratitude will attract more to be grateful for in your life.

____ /____ /____

COUNT YOUR BLESSINGS!

LIST 7 THINGS YOU ARE *grateful* FOR

Today I A.M. Grateful for

1. ______________________________

Because: ______________________________

____

2. ______________________________

Because: ______________________________

____

3. ______________________________

Because: ______________________________

____

4. ______________________________

Because: ______________________________

____

5. ______________________________

Because: ______________________________

____

6. ______________________________

Because: ______________________________

____

7. ______________________________

Because: ______________________________

____

Once you finish, go back and read everything and say to yourself or out loud: "Thank You God for this blessing" after each blessing. Having an attitude of gratitude will attract more to be grateful for in your life.

____ / ____ / ____

COUNT YOUR BLESSINGS!

LIST 7 THINGS YOU ARE *grateful* FOR

Today I A.M. Grateful for

1. ______________________________

Because: ______________________________

____

2. ______________________________

Because: ______________________________

____

3. ______________________________

Because: ______________________________

____

4. ______________________________

Because: ______________________________

____

5. ______________________________

Because: ______________________________

____

6. ______________________________

Because: ______________________________

____

7. ______________________________

Because: ______________________________

____

Once you finish, go back and read everything and say to yourself or out loud: "Thank You God for this blessing" after each blessing. Having an attitude of gratitude will attract more to be grateful for in your life.

____ / ____ / ____

COUNT YOUR BLESSINGS!

LIST 7 THINGS YOU ARE *grateful* FOR

Today I A.M. Grateful for

1. ____________________

Because: ____________________

2. ____________________

Because: ____________________

3. ____________________

Because: ____________________

4. ____________________

Because: ____________________

5. ____________________

Because: ____________________

6. ____________________

Because: ____________________

7. ____________________

Because: ____________________

Once you finish, go back and read everything and say to yourself or out loud: "Thank You God for this blessing" after each blessing. Having an attitude of gratitude will attract more to be grateful for in your life.

____ / ____ / ____

COUNT YOUR BLESSINGS!

LIST 7 THINGS YOU ARE *grateful* FOR

Today I A.M. Grateful for

1. ________________________________

Because: ________________________________

____

2. ________________________________

Because: ________________________________

____

3. ________________________________

Because: ________________________________

____

4. ________________________________

Because: ________________________________

____

5. ________________________________

Because: ________________________________

____

6. ________________________________

Because: ________________________________

____

7. ________________________________

Because: ________________________________

____

Once you finish, go back and read everything and say to yourself or out loud: "Thank You God for this blessing" after each blessing. Having an attitude of gratitude will attract more to be grateful for in your life.

____ /____ /____

COUNT YOUR BLESSINGS!

LIST 7 THINGS YOU ARE *grateful* FOR

Today I A.M. Grateful for

1. ______________________________

Because: ______________________________

____

2. ______________________________

Because: ______________________________

____

3. ______________________________

Because: ______________________________

____

4. ______________________________

Because: ______________________________

____

5. ______________________________

Because: ______________________________

____

6. ______________________________

Because: ______________________________

____

7. ______________________________

Because: ______________________________

____

Once you finish, go back and read everything and say to yourself or out loud: "Thank You God for this blessing" after each blessing. Having an attitude of gratitude will attract more to be grateful for in your life.

____ / ____ / ____

COUNT YOUR BLESSINGS!

LIST 7 THINGS YOU ARE *grateful* FOR

Today I A.M. Grateful for

1. ______________________________

Because: ______________________________

____

2. ______________________________

Because: ______________________________

____

3. ______________________________

Because: ______________________________

____

4. ______________________________

Because: ______________________________

____

5. ______________________________

Because: ______________________________

____

6. ______________________________

Because: ______________________________

____

7. ______________________________

Because: ______________________________

____

Once you finish, go back and read everything and say to yourself or out loud: "Thank You God for this blessing" after each blessing. Having an attitude of gratitude will attract more to be grateful for in your life.

____ /____ /____

COUNT YOUR BLESSINGS!

LIST 7 THINGS YOU ARE *grateful* FOR

Today I A.M. Grateful for

1. ______________________________

Because: ______________________________

____

2. ______________________________

Because: ______________________________

____

3. ______________________________

Because: ______________________________

____

4. ______________________________

Because: ______________________________

____

5. ______________________________

Because: ______________________________

____

6. ______________________________

Because: ______________________________

____

7. ______________________________

Because: ______________________________

____

Once you finish, go back and read everything and say to yourself or out loud: "Thank You God for this blessing" after each blessing. Having an attitude of gratitude will attract more to be grateful for in your life.

____ / ____ / ____

COUNT YOUR BLESSINGS!

LIST 7 THINGS YOU ARE *grateful* FOR

Today I A.M. Grateful for

1. ____________________

Because: ____________________

____

2. ____________________

Because: ____________________

____

3. ____________________

Because: ____________________

____

4. ____________________

Because: ____________________

____

5. ____________________

Because: ____________________

____

6. ____________________

Because: ____________________

____

7. ____________________

Because: ____________________

____

Once you finish, go back and read everything and say to yourself or out loud: "Thank You God for this blessing" after each blessing. Having an attitude of gratitude will attract more to be grateful for in your life.

Nothing and no one can stand in
the way of what is meant for you.

With God

anything is possible!
His timing is always perfect.

____ / ____ / ____

COUNT YOUR BLESSINGS!

LIST 7 THINGS YOU ARE *grateful* FOR

Today I A.M. Grateful for

1. ______________________________

Because: ______________________________

____

2. ______________________________

Because: ______________________________

____

3. ______________________________

Because: ______________________________

____

4. ______________________________

Because: ______________________________

____

5. ______________________________

Because: ______________________________

____

6. ______________________________

Because: ______________________________

____

7. ______________________________

Because: ______________________________

____

Once you finish, go back and read everything and say to yourself or out loud: "Thank You God for this blessing" after each blessing. Having an attitude of gratitude will attract more to be grateful for in your life.

____ /____ /____

COUNT YOUR BLESSINGS!

LIST 7 THINGS YOU ARE *grateful* FOR

Today I A.M. Grateful for

1. ____________________

Because: ____________________

____

2. ____________________

Because: ____________________

____

3. ____________________

Because: ____________________

____

4. ____________________

Because: ____________________

____

5. ____________________

Because: ____________________

____

6. ____________________

Because: ____________________

____

7. ____________________

Because: ____________________

____

Once you finish, go back and read everything and say to yourself or out loud: "Thank You God for this blessing" after each blessing. Having an attitude of gratitude will attract more to be grateful for in your life.

____ / ____ / ____

COUNT YOUR BLESSINGS!

LIST 7 THINGS YOU ARE *grateful* FOR

Today I A.M. Grateful for

1. ____________________
Because: ____________________

2. ____________________
Because: ____________________

3. ____________________
Because: ____________________

4. ____________________
Because: ____________________

5. ____________________
Because: ____________________

6. ____________________
Because: ____________________

7. ____________________
Because: ____________________

Once you finish, go back and read everything and say to yourself or out loud: "Thank You God for this blessing" after each blessing. Having an attitude of gratitude will attract more to be grateful for in your life.

____ /____ /____

COUNT YOUR BLESSINGS!

LIST 7 THINGS YOU ARE *grateful* FOR

Today I A.M. Grateful for

1. ______________________________

Because: ______________________________

____

2. ______________________________

Because: ______________________________

____

3. ______________________________

Because: ______________________________

____

4. ______________________________

Because: ______________________________

____

5. ______________________________

Because: ______________________________

____

6. ______________________________

Because: ______________________________

____

7. ______________________________

Because: ______________________________

____

Once you finish, go back and read everything and say to yourself or out loud: "Thank You God for this blessing" after each blessing. Having an attitude of gratitude will attract more to be grateful for in your life.

____ / ____ / ____

COUNT YOUR BLESSINGS!

LIST 7 THINGS YOU ARE *grateful* FOR

Today I A.M. Grateful for

1. ____________________

Because: ____________________

____

2. ____________________

Because: ____________________

____

3. ____________________

Because: ____________________

____

4. ____________________

Because: ____________________

____

5. ____________________

Because: ____________________

____

6. ____________________

Because: ____________________

____

7. ____________________

Because: ____________________

____

Once you finish, go back and read everything and say to yourself or out loud: "Thank You God for this blessing" after each blessing. Having an attitude of gratitude will attract more to be grateful for in your life.

____ / ____ / ____

COUNT YOUR BLESSINGS!

LIST 7 THINGS YOU ARE *grateful* FOR

Today I A.M. Grateful for

1. ______________________

Because: ______________________

____

2. ______________________

Because: ______________________

____

3. ______________________

Because: ______________________

____

4. ______________________

Because: ______________________

____

5. ______________________

Because: ______________________

____

6. ______________________

Because: ______________________

____

7. ______________________

Because: ______________________

____

Once you finish, go back and read everything and say to yourself or out loud: "Thank You God for this blessing" after each blessing. Having an attitude of gratitude will attract more to be grateful for in your life.

____ /____ /____

COUNT YOUR BLESSINGS!

LIST 7 THINGS YOU ARE *grateful* FOR

Today I A.M. Grateful for

1. ____________________

Because: ____________________

____

2. ____________________

Because: ____________________

____

3. ____________________

Because: ____________________

____

4. ____________________

Because: ____________________

____

5. ____________________

Because: ____________________

____

6. ____________________

Because: ____________________

____

7. ____________________

Because: ____________________

____

Once you finish, go back and read everything and say to yourself or out loud: "Thank You God for this blessing" after each blessing. Having an attitude of gratitude will attract more to be grateful for in your life.

____ /____ /____

COUNT YOUR BLESSINGS!

LIST 7 THINGS YOU ARE *grateful* FOR

Today I A.M. Grateful for

1. ____

Because: ____

____

2. ____

Because: ____

____

3. ____

Because: ____

____

4. ____

Because: ____

____

5. ____

Because: ____

____

6. ____

Because: ____

____

7. ____

Because: ____

____

Once you finish, go back and read everything and say to yourself or out loud: "Thank You God for this blessing" after each blessing. Having an attitude of gratitude will attract more to be grateful for in your life.

____ / ____ / ____

COUNT YOUR BLESSINGS!

LIST 7 THINGS YOU ARE *grateful* FOR

Today I A.M. Grateful for

1. ____

Because: ____

____

2. ____

Because: ____

____

3. ____

Because: ____

____

4. ____

Because: ____

____

5. ____

Because: ____

____

6. ____

Because: ____

____

7. ____

Because: ____

____

Once you finish, go back and read everything and say to yourself or out loud: "Thank You God for this blessing" after each blessing. Having an attitude of gratitude will attract more to be grateful for in your life.

____ /____ /____

COUNT YOUR BLESSINGS!

LIST 7 THINGS YOU ARE *grateful* FOR

Today I A.M. Grateful for

1. ______________________________
Because: ______________________________
____

2. ______________________________
Because: ______________________________
____

3. ______________________________
Because: ______________________________
____

4. ______________________________
Because: ______________________________
____

5. ______________________________
Because: ______________________________
____

6. ______________________________
Because: ______________________________
____

7. ______________________________
Because: ______________________________
____

Once you finish, go back and read everything and say to yourself or out loud: "Thank You God for this blessing" after each blessing. Having an attitude of gratitude will attract more to be grateful for in your life.

____ / ____ / ____

COUNT YOUR BLESSINGS!

LIST 7 THINGS YOU ARE *grateful* FOR

Today I A.M. Grateful for

1. ____________________

Because: ____________________

____

2. ____________________

Because: ____________________

____

3. ____________________

Because: ____________________

____

4. ____________________

Because: ____________________

____

5. ____________________

Because: ____________________

____

6. ____________________

Because: ____________________

____

7. ____________________

Because: ____________________

____

Once you finish, go back and read everything and say to yourself or out loud: "Thank You God for this blessing" after each blessing. Having an attitude of gratitude will attract more to be grateful for in your life.

_____ /_____ /_____

COUNT YOUR BLESSINGS!

LIST 7 THINGS YOU ARE *grateful* FOR

Today I A.M. Grateful for

1. ______________________________

Because: ______________________________

____

2. ______________________________

Because: ______________________________

____

3. ______________________________

Because: ______________________________

____

4. ______________________________

Because: ______________________________

____

5. ______________________________

Because: ______________________________

____

6. ______________________________

Because: ______________________________

____

7. ______________________________

Because: ______________________________

____

Once you finish, go back and read everything and say to yourself or out loud: "Thank You God for this blessing" after each blessing. Having an attitude of gratitude will attract more to be grateful for in your life.

____ /____ /____

COUNT YOUR BLESSINGS!

LIST 7 THINGS YOU ARE *grateful* FOR

Today I A.M. Grateful for

1. ______________________________

Because: ______________________________

____

2. ______________________________

Because: ______________________________

____

3. ______________________________

Because: ______________________________

____

4. ______________________________

Because: ______________________________

____

5. ______________________________

Because: ______________________________

____

6. ______________________________

Because: ______________________________

____

7. ______________________________

Because: ______________________________

____

Once you finish, go back and read everything and say to yourself or out loud: "Thank You God for this blessing" after each blessing. Having an attitude of gratitude will attract more to be grateful for in your life.

____ / ____ / ____

COUNT YOUR BLESSINGS!

LIST 7 THINGS YOU ARE *grateful* FOR

Today I A.M. Grateful for

1. ______________________________

Because: ______________________________

____

2. ______________________________

Because: ______________________________

____

3. ______________________________

Because: ______________________________

____

4. ______________________________

Because: ______________________________

____

5. ______________________________

Because: ______________________________

____

6. ______________________________

Because: ______________________________

____

7. ______________________________

Because: ______________________________

____

Once you finish, go back and read everything and say to yourself or out loud: "Thank You God for this blessing" after each blessing. Having an attitude of gratitude will attract more to be grateful for in your life.

____ / ____ / ____

COUNT YOUR BLESSINGS!

LIST 7 THINGS YOU ARE *grateful* FOR

Today I A.M. Grateful for

1. ______________________________

Because: ______________________________

____

2. ______________________________

Because: ______________________________

____

3. ______________________________

Because: ______________________________

____

4. ______________________________

Because: ______________________________

____

5. ______________________________

Because: ______________________________

____

6. ______________________________

Because: ______________________________

____

7. ______________________________

Because: ______________________________

____

Once you finish, go back and read everything and say to yourself or out loud: "Thank You God for this blessing" after each blessing. Having an attitude of gratitude will attract more to be grateful for in your life.

____ / ____ / ____

COUNT YOUR BLESSINGS!

LIST 7 THINGS YOU ARE *grateful* FOR

Today I A.M. Grateful for

1. __________

Because: __________

2. __________

Because: __________

3. __________

Because: __________

4. __________

Because: __________

5. __________

Because: __________

6. __________

Because: __________

7. __________

Because: __________

Once you finish, go back and read everything and say to yourself or out loud: "Thank You God for this blessing" after each blessing. Having an attitude of gratitude will attract more to be grateful for in your life.

____ / ____ / ____

COUNT YOUR BLESSINGS!

LIST 7 THINGS YOU ARE *grateful* FOR

Today I A.M. Grateful for

1. ____________________

Because: ____________________

____

2. ____________________

Because: ____________________

____

3. ____________________

Because: ____________________

____

4. ____________________

Because: ____________________

____

5. ____________________

Because: ____________________

____

6. ____________________

Because: ____________________

____

7. ____________________

Because: ____________________

____

Once you finish, go back and read everything and say to yourself or out loud: "Thank You God for this blessing" after each blessing. Having an attitude of gratitude will attract more to be grateful for in your life.

____ / ____ / ____

COUNT YOUR BLESSINGS!

LIST 7 THINGS YOU ARE *grateful* FOR

Today I A.M. Grateful for

1. ____________________
Because: ____________________

2. ____________________
Because: ____________________

3. ____________________
Because: ____________________

4. ____________________
Because: ____________________

5. ____________________
Because: ____________________

6. ____________________
Because: ____________________

7. ____________________
Because: ____________________

Once you finish, go back and read everything and say to yourself or out loud: "Thank You God for this blessing" after each blessing. Having an attitude of gratitude will attract more to be grateful for in your life.

____ / ____ / ____

COUNT YOUR BLESSINGS!

LIST 7 THINGS YOU ARE *grateful* FOR

Today I A.M. Grateful for

1. ____________________

Because: ____________________

____

2. ____________________

Because: ____________________

____

3. ____________________

Because: ____________________

____

4. ____________________

Because: ____________________

____

5. ____________________

Because: ____________________

____

6. ____________________

Because: ____________________

____

7. ____________________

Because: ____________________

____

Once you finish, go back and read everything and say to yourself or out loud: "Thank You God for this blessing" after each blessing. Having an attitude of gratitude will attract more to be grateful for in your life.

____ /____ /____

COUNT YOUR BLESSINGS!

LIST 7 THINGS YOU ARE *grateful* FOR

Today I A.M. Grateful for

1. ____________________

Because: ____________________

____

2. ____________________

Because: ____________________

____

3. ____________________

Because: ____________________

____

4. ____________________

Because: ____________________

____

5. ____________________

Because: ____________________

____

6. ____________________

Because: ____________________

____

7. ____________________

Because: ____________________

____

Once you finish, go back and read everything and say to yourself or out loud: "Thank You God for this blessing" after each blessing. Having an attitude of gratitude will attract more to be grateful for in your life.

____ / ____ / ____

COUNT YOUR BLESSINGS!

LIST 7 THINGS YOU ARE *grateful* FOR

Today I A.M. Grateful for

1. ______________________________

Because: ______________________________

____

2. ______________________________

Because: ______________________________

____

3. ______________________________

Because: ______________________________

____

4. ______________________________

Because: ______________________________

____

5. ______________________________

Because: ______________________________

____

6. ______________________________

Because: ______________________________

____

7. ______________________________

Because: ______________________________

____

Once you finish, go back and read everything and say to yourself or out loud: "Thank You God for this blessing" after each blessing. Having an attitude of gratitude will attract more to be grateful for in your life.

____ /____ /____

COUNT YOUR BLESSINGS!

LIST 7 THINGS YOU ARE *grateful* FOR

Today I A.M. Grateful for

1. ____________________

Because: ____________________

____

2. ____________________

Because: ____________________

____

3. ____________________

Because: ____________________

____

4. ____________________

Because: ____________________

____

5. ____________________

Because: ____________________

____

6. ____________________

Because: ____________________

____

7. ____________________

Because: ____________________

____

Once you finish, go back and read everything and say to yourself or out loud: "Thank You God for this blessing" after each blessing. Having an attitude of gratitude will attract more to be grateful for in your life.

____ / ____ / ____

COUNT YOUR BLESSINGS!

LIST 7 THINGS YOU ARE *grateful* FOR

Today I A.M. Grateful for

1. ____________________

Because: ____________________

____

2. ____________________

Because: ____________________

____

3. ____________________

Because: ____________________

____

4. ____________________

Because: ____________________

____

5. ____________________

Because: ____________________

____

6. ____________________

Because: ____________________

____

7. ____________________

Because: ____________________

____

Once you finish, go back and read everything and say to yourself or out loud: "Thank You God for this blessing" after each blessing. Having an attitude of gratitude will attract more to be grateful for in your life.

____ /____ /____

COUNT YOUR BLESSINGS!

LIST 7 THINGS YOU ARE *grateful* FOR

Today I A.M. Grateful for

1. ______________________________

Because: ______________________________

____

2. ______________________________

Because: ______________________________

____

3. ______________________________

Because: ______________________________

____

4. ______________________________

Because: ______________________________

____

5. ______________________________

Because: ______________________________

____

6. ______________________________

Because: ______________________________

____

7. ______________________________

Because: ______________________________

____

Once you finish, go back and read everything and say to yourself or out loud: "Thank You God for this blessing" after each blessing. Having an attitude of gratitude will attract more to be grateful for in your life.

____ / ____ / ____

COUNT YOUR BLESSINGS!

LIST 7 THINGS YOU ARE *grateful* FOR

Today I A.M. Grateful for

1. ____________________

Because: ____________________

____

2. ____________________

Because: ____________________

____

3. ____________________

Because: ____________________

____

4. ____________________

Because: ____________________

____

5. ____________________

Because: ____________________

____

6. ____________________

Because: ____________________

____

7. ____________________

Because: ____________________

____

Once you finish, go back and read everything and say to yourself or out loud: "Thank You God for this blessing" after each blessing. Having an attitude of gratitude will attract more to be grateful for in your life.

____ /____ /____

COUNT YOUR BLESSINGS!

LIST 7 THINGS YOU ARE *grateful* FOR

Today I A.M. Grateful for

1. ______________________________

Because: ______________________________

____

2. ______________________________

Because: ______________________________

____

3. ______________________________

Because: ______________________________

____

4. ______________________________

Because: ______________________________

____

5. ______________________________

Because: ______________________________

____

6. ______________________________

Because: ______________________________

____

7. ______________________________

Because: ______________________________

____

Once you finish, go back and read everything and say to yourself or out loud: "Thank You God for this blessing" after each blessing. Having an attitude of gratitude will attract more to be grateful for in your life.

____ /____ /____

COUNT YOUR BLESSINGS!

LIST 7 THINGS YOU ARE *grateful* FOR

Today I A.M. Grateful for

1. ______________________________

Because: ______________________________

____

2. ______________________________

Because: ______________________________

____

3. ______________________________

Because: ______________________________

____

4. ______________________________

Because: ______________________________

____

5. ______________________________

Because: ______________________________

____

6. ______________________________

Because: ______________________________

____

7. ______________________________

Because: ______________________________

____

Once you finish, go back and read everything and say to yourself or out loud: "Thank You God for this blessing" after each blessing. Having an attitude of gratitude will attract more to be grateful for in your life.

____ /____ /____

COUNT YOUR BLESSINGS!

LIST 7 THINGS YOU ARE *grateful* FOR

Today I A.M. Grateful for

1. ______________________________

Because: ______________________________

____

2. ______________________________

Because: ______________________________

____

3. ______________________________

Because: ______________________________

____

4. ______________________________

Because: ______________________________

____

5. ______________________________

Because: ______________________________

____

6. ______________________________

Because: ______________________________

____

7. ______________________________

Because: ______________________________

____

Once you finish, go back and read everything and say to yourself or out loud: "Thank You God for this blessing" after each blessing. Having an attitude of gratitude will attract more to be grateful for in your life.

____ / ____ / ____

COUNT YOUR BLESSINGS!

LIST 7 THINGS YOU ARE *grateful* FOR

Today I A.M. Grateful for

1. ____________________

Because: ____________________

2. ____________________

Because: ____________________

3. ____________________

Because: ____________________

4. ____________________

Because: ____________________

5. ____________________

Because: ____________________

6. ____________________

Because: ____________________

7. ____________________

Because: ____________________

Once you finish, go back and read everything and say to yourself or out loud: "Thank You God for this blessing" after each blessing. Having an attitude of gratitude will attract more to be grateful for in your life.

____ /____ /____

COUNT YOUR BLESSINGS!

LIST 7 THINGS YOU ARE *grateful* FOR

Today I A.M. Grateful for

1. ____________________

Because: ____________________

____

2. ____________________

Because: ____________________

____

3. ____________________

Because: ____________________

____

4. ____________________

Because: ____________________

____

5. ____________________

Because: ____________________

____

6. ____________________

Because: ____________________

____

7. ____________________

Because: ____________________

____

Once you finish, go back and read everything and say to yourself or out loud: "Thank You God for this blessing" after each blessing. Having an attitude of gratitude will attract more to be grateful for in your life.

____ / ____ / ____

COUNT YOUR BLESSINGS!

LIST 7 THINGS YOU ARE *grateful* FOR

Today I A.M. Grateful for

1. ______________________________

Because: ______________________________

____

2. ______________________________

Because: ______________________________

____

3. ______________________________

Because: ______________________________

____

4. ______________________________

Because: ______________________________

____

5. ______________________________

Because: ______________________________

____

6. ______________________________

Because: ______________________________

____

7. ______________________________

Because: ______________________________

____

Once you finish, go back and read everything and say to yourself or out loud: "Thank You God for this blessing" after each blessing. Having an attitude of gratitude will attract more to be grateful for in your life.

____ /____ /____

COUNT YOUR BLESSINGS!

LIST 7 THINGS YOU ARE *grateful* FOR

Today I A.M. Grateful for

1. ____________________

Because: ____________________

____

2. ____________________

Because: ____________________

____

3. ____________________

Because: ____________________

____

4. ____________________

Because: ____________________

____

5. ____________________

Because: ____________________

____

6. ____________________

Because: ____________________

____

7. ____________________

Because: ____________________

____

Once you finish, go back and read everything and say to yourself or out loud: "Thank You God for this blessing" after each blessing. Having an attitude of gratitude will attract more to be grateful for in your life.

____ / ____ / ____

COUNT YOUR BLESSINGS!

LIST 7 THINGS YOU ARE *grateful* FOR

Today I A.M. Grateful for

1. ____

Because: ____

____

2. ____

Because: ____

____

3. ____

Because: ____

____

4. ____

Because: ____

____

5. ____

Because: ____

____

6. ____

Because: ____

____

7. ____

Because: ____

____

Once you finish, go back and read everything and say to yourself or out loud: "Thank You God for this blessing" after each blessing. Having an attitude of gratitude will attract more to be grateful for in your life.

____ /____ /____

COUNT YOUR BLESSINGS!

LIST 7 THINGS YOU ARE *grateful* FOR

Today I A.M. Grateful for

1. ________________________________

Because: ________________________________

____

2. ________________________________

Because: ________________________________

____

3. ________________________________

Because: ________________________________

____

4. ________________________________

Because: ________________________________

____

5. ________________________________

Because: ________________________________

____

6. ________________________________

Because: ________________________________

____

7. ________________________________

Because: ________________________________

____

Once you finish, go back and read everything and say to yourself or out loud: "Thank You God for this blessing" after each blessing. Having an attitude of gratitude will attract more to be grateful for in your life.

____ /____ /____

COUNT YOUR BLESSINGS!

LIST 7 THINGS YOU ARE *grateful* FOR

Today I A.M. Grateful for

1. ____________________

Because: ____________________

____

2. ____________________

Because: ____________________

____

3. ____________________

Because: ____________________

____

4. ____________________

Because: ____________________

____

5. ____________________

Because: ____________________

____

6. ____________________

Because: ____________________

____

7. ____________________

Because: ____________________

____

Once you finish, go back and read everything and say to yourself or out loud: "Thank You God for this blessing" after each blessing. Having an attitude of gratitude will attract more to be grateful for in your life.

When the devil keeps asking you to
keep looking at your past,
there's something in your

future

that he doesn't want you to see

____ /____ /____

COUNT YOUR BLESSINGS!

LIST 7 THINGS YOU ARE *grateful* FOR

Today I A.M. Grateful for

1. ______________________________

Because: ______________________________

____

2. ______________________________

Because: ______________________________

____

3. ______________________________

Because: ______________________________

____

4. ______________________________

Because: ______________________________

____

5. ______________________________

Because: ______________________________

____

6. ______________________________

Because: ______________________________

____

7. ______________________________

Because: ______________________________

____

Once you finish, go back and read everything and say to yourself or out loud: "Thank You God for this blessing" after each blessing. Having an attitude of gratitude will attract more to be grateful for in your life.

____ /____ /____

COUNT YOUR BLESSINGS!

LIST 7 THINGS YOU ARE *grateful* FOR

Today I A.M. Grateful for

1. ______________________________

Because: ______________________________

____

2. ______________________________

Because: ______________________________

____

3. ______________________________

Because: ______________________________

____

4. ______________________________

Because: ______________________________

____

5. ______________________________

Because: ______________________________

____

6. ______________________________

Because: ______________________________

____

7. ______________________________

Because: ______________________________

____

Once you finish, go back and read everything and say to yourself or out loud: "Thank You God for this blessing" after each blessing. Having an attitude of gratitude will attract more to be grateful for in your life.

____ /____ /____

COUNT YOUR BLESSINGS!

LIST 7 THINGS YOU ARE *grateful* FOR

Today I A.M. Grateful for

1. ______________________________

Because: ______________________________

____

2. ______________________________

Because: ______________________________

____

3. ______________________________

Because: ______________________________

____

4. ______________________________

Because: ______________________________

____

5. ______________________________

Because: ______________________________

____

6. ______________________________

Because: ______________________________

____

7. ______________________________

Because: ______________________________

____

Once you finish, go back and read everything and say to yourself or out loud: "Thank You God for this blessing" after each blessing. Having an attitude of gratitude will attract more to be grateful for in your life.

____ / ____ / ____

COUNT YOUR BLESSINGS!

LIST 7 THINGS YOU ARE *grateful* FOR

Today I A.M. Grateful for

1. ____________________

Because: ____________________

2. ____________________

Because: ____________________

3. ____________________

Because: ____________________

4. ____________________

Because: ____________________

5. ____________________

Because: ____________________

6. ____________________

Because: ____________________

7. ____________________

Because: ____________________

Once you finish, go back and read everything and say to yourself or out loud: "Thank You God for this blessing" after each blessing. Having an attitude of gratitude will attract more to be grateful for in your life.

____ / ____ / ____

COUNT YOUR BLESSINGS!

LIST 7 THINGS YOU ARE *grateful* FOR

Today I A.M. Grateful for

1. ____________________

Because: ____________________

2. ____________________

Because: ____________________

3. ____________________

Because: ____________________

4. ____________________

Because: ____________________

5. ____________________

Because: ____________________

6. ____________________

Because: ____________________

7. ____________________

Because: ____________________

Once you finish, go back and read everything and say to yourself or out loud: "Thank You God for this blessing" after each blessing. Having an attitude of gratitude will attract more to be grateful for in your life.

____ /____ /____

COUNT YOUR BLESSINGS!

LIST 7 THINGS YOU ARE *grateful* FOR

Today I A.M. Grateful for

1. ________________________________

Because: ________________________________

____

2. ________________________________

Because: ________________________________

____

3. ________________________________

Because: ________________________________

____

4. ________________________________

Because: ________________________________

____

5. ________________________________

Because: ________________________________

____

6. ________________________________

Because: ________________________________

____

7. ________________________________

Because: ________________________________

____

Once you finish, go back and read everything and say to yourself or out loud: "Thank You God for this blessing" after each blessing. Having an attitude of gratitude will attract more to be grateful for in your life.

____ / ____ / ____

COUNT YOUR BLESSINGS!

LIST 7 THINGS YOU ARE *grateful* FOR

Today I A.M. Grateful for

1. ______________________________

Because: ______________________________

____

2. ______________________________

Because: ______________________________

____

3. ______________________________

Because: ______________________________

____

4. ______________________________

Because: ______________________________

____

5. ______________________________

Because: ______________________________

____

6. ______________________________

Because: ______________________________

____

7. ______________________________

Because: ______________________________

____

Once you finish, go back and read everything and say to yourself or out loud: "Thank You God for this blessing" after each blessing. Having an attitude of gratitude will attract more to be grateful for in your life.

____ /____ /____

COUNT YOUR BLESSINGS!

LIST 7 THINGS YOU ARE *grateful* FOR

Today I A.M. Grateful for

1. ____________________

Because: ____________________

____

2. ____________________

Because: ____________________

____

3. ____________________

Because: ____________________

____

4. ____________________

Because: ____________________

____

5. ____________________

Because: ____________________

____

6. ____________________

Because: ____________________

____

7. ____________________

Because: ____________________

____

Once you finish, go back and read everything and say to yourself or out loud: "Thank You God for this blessing" after each blessing. Having an attitude of gratitude will attract more to be grateful for in your life.

____ / ____ / ____

COUNT YOUR BLESSINGS!

LIST 7 THINGS YOU ARE *grateful* FOR

Today I A.M. Grateful for

1. ____________________

Because: ____________________

____

2. ____________________

Because: ____________________

____

3. ____________________

Because: ____________________

____

4. ____________________

Because: ____________________

____

5. ____________________

Because: ____________________

____

6. ____________________

Because: ____________________

____

7. ____________________

Because: ____________________

____

Once you finish, go back and read everything and say to yourself or out loud: "Thank You God for this blessing" after each blessing. Having an attitude of gratitude will attract more to be grateful for in your life.

____ / ____ / ____

COUNT YOUR BLESSINGS!

LIST 7 THINGS YOU ARE *grateful* FOR

Today I A.M. Grateful for

1. ________________________________

Because: ________________________________

____

2. ________________________________

Because: ________________________________

____

3. ________________________________

Because: ________________________________

____

4. ________________________________

Because: ________________________________

____

5. ________________________________

Because: ________________________________

____

6. ________________________________

Because: ________________________________

____

7. ________________________________

Because: ________________________________

____

Once you finish, go back and read everything and say to yourself or out loud: "Thank You God for this blessing" after each blessing. Having an attitude of gratitude will attract more to be grateful for in your life.

____ / ____ / ____

COUNT YOUR BLESSINGS!

LIST 7 THINGS YOU ARE *grateful* FOR

Today I A.M. Grateful for

1. ____________________

Because: ____________________

____

2. ____________________

Because: ____________________

____

3. ____________________

Because: ____________________

____

4. ____________________

Because: ____________________

____

5. ____________________

Because: ____________________

____

6. ____________________

Because: ____________________

____

7. ____________________

Because: ____________________

____

Once you finish, go back and read everything and say to yourself or out loud: "Thank You God for this blessing" after each blessing. Having an attitude of gratitude will attract more to be grateful for in your life.

____ / ____ / ____

COUNT YOUR BLESSINGS!

LIST 7 THINGS YOU ARE *grateful* FOR

Today I A.M. Grateful for

1. ______________________

Because: ______________________

____

2. ______________________

Because: ______________________

____

3. ______________________

Because: ______________________

____

4. ______________________

Because: ______________________

____

5. ______________________

Because: ______________________

____

6. ______________________

Because: ______________________

____

7. ______________________

Because: ______________________

____

Once you finish, go back and read everything and say to yourself or out loud: "Thank You God for this blessing" after each blessing. Having an attitude of gratitude will attract more to be grateful for in your life.

____ /____ /____

COUNT YOUR BLESSINGS!

LIST 7 THINGS YOU ARE *grateful* FOR

Today I A.M. Grateful for

1. ____________________

Because: ____________________

____

2. ____________________

Because: ____________________

____

3. ____________________

Because: ____________________

____

4. ____________________

Because: ____________________

____

5. ____________________

Because: ____________________

____

6. ____________________

Because: ____________________

____

7. ____________________

Because: ____________________

____

Once you finish, go back and read everything and say to yourself or out loud: "Thank You God for this blessing" after each blessing. Having an attitude of gratitude will attract more to be grateful for in your life.

____ /____ /____

COUNT YOUR BLESSINGS!

LIST 7 THINGS YOU ARE *grateful* FOR

Today I A.M. Grateful for

1. ____________________

Because: ____________________

____

2. ____________________

Because: ____________________

____

3. ____________________

Because: ____________________

____

4. ____________________

Because: ____________________

____

5. ____________________

Because: ____________________

____

6. ____________________

Because: ____________________

____

7. ____________________

Because: ____________________

____

Once you finish, go back and read everything and say to yourself or out loud: "Thank You God for this blessing" after each blessing. Having an attitude of gratitude will attract more to be grateful for in your life.

____ /____ /____

COUNT YOUR BLESSINGS!

LIST 7 THINGS YOU ARE *grateful* FOR

Today I A.M. Grateful for

1. ______________________________

Because: ______________________________

____

2. ______________________________

Because: ______________________________

____

3. ______________________________

Because: ______________________________

____

4. ______________________________

Because: ______________________________

____

5. ______________________________

Because: ______________________________

____

6. ______________________________

Because: ______________________________

____

7. ______________________________

Because: ______________________________

____

Once you finish, go back and read everything and say to yourself or out loud: "Thank You God for this blessing" after each blessing. Having an attitude of gratitude will attract more to be grateful for in your life.

____ / ____ / ____

COUNT YOUR BLESSINGS!

LIST 7 THINGS YOU ARE *grateful* FOR

Today I A.M. Grateful for

1. ____________________

Because: ____________________

____

2. ____________________

Because: ____________________

____

3. ____________________

Because: ____________________

____

4. ____________________

Because: ____________________

____

5. ____________________

Because: ____________________

____

6. ____________________

Because: ____________________

____

7. ____________________

Because: ____________________

____

Once you finish, go back and read everything and say to yourself or out loud: "Thank You God for this blessing" after each blessing. Having an attitude of gratitude will attract more to be grateful for in your life.

___ / ___ / ___

COUNT YOUR BLESSINGS!

LIST 7 THINGS YOU ARE *grateful* FOR

Today I A.M. Grateful for

1. ______________________________

Because: ______________________________

____

2. ______________________________

Because: ______________________________

____

3. ______________________________

Because: ______________________________

____

4. ______________________________

Because: ______________________________

____

5. ______________________________

Because: ______________________________

____

6. ______________________________

Because: ______________________________

____

7. ______________________________

Because: ______________________________

____

Once you finish, go back and read everything and say to yourself or out loud: "Thank You God for this blessing" after each blessing. Having an attitude of gratitude will attract more to be grateful for in your life.

____ / ____ / ____

COUNT YOUR BLESSINGS!

LIST 7 THINGS YOU ARE *grateful* FOR

Today I A.M. Grateful for

1. ______________________________

Because: ______________________________

____

2. ______________________________

Because: ______________________________

____

3. ______________________________

Because: ______________________________

____

4. ______________________________

Because: ______________________________

____

5. ______________________________

Because: ______________________________

____

6. ______________________________

Because: ______________________________

____

7. ______________________________

Because: ______________________________

____

Once you finish, go back and read everything and say to yourself or out loud: "Thank You God for this blessing" after each blessing. Having an attitude of gratitude will attract more to be grateful for in your life.

____ / ____ / ____

COUNT YOUR BLESSINGS!

LIST 7 THINGS YOU ARE *grateful* FOR

Today I A.M. Grateful for

1. ______________________________

Because: ______________________________

____

2. ______________________________

Because: ______________________________

____

3. ______________________________

Because: ______________________________

____

4. ______________________________

Because: ______________________________

____

5. ______________________________

Because: ______________________________

____

6. ______________________________

Because: ______________________________

____

7. ______________________________

Because: ______________________________

____

Once you finish, go back and read everything and say to yourself or out loud: "Thank You God for this blessing" after each blessing. Having an attitude of gratitude will attract more to be grateful for in your life.

____ /____ /____

COUNT YOUR BLESSINGS!

LIST 7 THINGS YOU ARE *grateful* FOR

Today I A.M. Grateful for

1. ______________________________

Because: ______________________________

____

2. ______________________________

Because: ______________________________

____

3. ______________________________

Because: ______________________________

____

4. ______________________________

Because: ______________________________

____

5. ______________________________

Because: ______________________________

____

6. ______________________________

Because: ______________________________

____

7. ______________________________

Because: ______________________________

____

Once you finish, go back and read everything and say to yourself or out loud: "Thank You God for this blessing" after each blessing. Having an attitude of gratitude will attract more to be grateful for in your life.

____ /____ /____

COUNT YOUR BLESSINGS!

LIST 7 THINGS YOU ARE *grateful* FOR

Today I A.M. Grateful for

1. ______________________________

Because: ______________________________

____

2. ______________________________

Because: ______________________________

____

3. ______________________________

Because: ______________________________

____

4. ______________________________

Because: ______________________________

____

5. ______________________________

Because: ______________________________

____

6. ______________________________

Because: ______________________________

____

7. ______________________________

Because: ______________________________

____

Once you finish, go back and read everything and say to yourself or out loud: "Thank You God for this blessing" after each blessing. Having an attitude of gratitude will attract more to be grateful for in your life.

____ / ____ / ____

COUNT YOUR BLESSINGS!

LIST 7 THINGS YOU ARE *grateful* FOR

Today I A.M. Grateful for

1. ________________________________

Because: ________________________________

____

2. ________________________________

Because: ________________________________

____

3. ________________________________

Because: ________________________________

____

4. ________________________________

Because: ________________________________

____

5. ________________________________

Because: ________________________________

____

6. ________________________________

Because: ________________________________

____

7. ________________________________

Because: ________________________________

____

Once you finish, go back and read everything and say to yourself or out loud: "Thank You God for this blessing" after each blessing. Having an attitude of gratitude will attract more to be grateful for in your life.

____ / ____ / ____

COUNT YOUR BLESSINGS!

LIST 7 THINGS YOU ARE *grateful* FOR

Today I A.M. Grateful for

1. ____________________

Because: ____________________

2. ____________________

Because: ____________________

3. ____________________

Because: ____________________

4. ____________________

Because: ____________________

5. ____________________

Because: ____________________

6. ____________________

Because: ____________________

7. ____________________

Because: ____________________

Once you finish, go back and read everything and say to yourself or out loud: "Thank You God for this blessing" after each blessing. Having an attitude of gratitude will attract more to be grateful for in your life.

____ /____ /____

COUNT YOUR BLESSINGS!

LIST 7 THINGS YOU ARE *grateful* FOR

Today I A.M. Grateful for

1. ____________________

Because: ____________________

____

2. ____________________

Because: ____________________

____

3. ____________________

Because: ____________________

____

4. ____________________

Because: ____________________

____

5. ____________________

Because: ____________________

____

6. ____________________

Because: ____________________

____

7. ____________________

Because: ____________________

____

Once you finish, go back and read everything and say to yourself or out loud: "Thank You God for this blessing" after each blessing. Having an attitude of gratitude will attract more to be grateful for in your life.

___ / ___ / ___

COUNT YOUR BLESSINGS!

LIST 7 THINGS YOU ARE *grateful* FOR

Today I A.M. Grateful for

1. ______________________

Because: ______________________

____

2. ______________________

Because: ______________________

____

3. ______________________

Because: ______________________

____

4. ______________________

Because: ______________________

____

5. ______________________

Because: ______________________

____

6. ______________________

Because: ______________________

____

7. ______________________

Because: ______________________

____

Once you finish, go back and read everything and say to yourself or out loud: "Thank You God for this blessing" after each blessing. Having an attitude of gratitude will attract more to be grateful for in your life.

____ / ____ / ____

COUNT YOUR BLESSINGS!

LIST 7 THINGS YOU ARE *grateful* FOR

Today I A.M. Grateful for

1. ____________________

Because: ____________________

____

2. ____________________

Because: ____________________

____

3. ____________________

Because: ____________________

____

4. ____________________

Because: ____________________

____

5. ____________________

Because: ____________________

____

6. ____________________

Because: ____________________

____

7. ____________________

Because: ____________________

____

Once you finish, go back and read everything and say to yourself or out loud: "Thank You God for this blessing" after each blessing. Having an attitude of gratitude will attract more to be grateful for in your life.

____ /____ /____

COUNT YOUR BLESSINGS!

LIST 7 THINGS YOU ARE *grateful* FOR

Today I A.M. Grateful for

1. ____________________

Because: ____________________

____

2. ____________________

Because: ____________________

____

3. ____________________

Because: ____________________

____

4. ____________________

Because: ____________________

____

5. ____________________

Because: ____________________

____

6. ____________________

Because: ____________________

____

7. ____________________

Because: ____________________

____

Once you finish, go back and read everything and say to yourself or out loud: "Thank You God for this blessing" after each blessing. Having an attitude of gratitude will attract more to be grateful for in your life.

____ /____ /____

COUNT YOUR BLESSINGS!

LIST 7 THINGS YOU ARE *grateful* FOR

Today I A.M. Grateful for

1. ______________________________

Because: ______________________________

____

2. ______________________________

Because: ______________________________

____

3. ______________________________

Because: ______________________________

____

4. ______________________________

Because: ______________________________

____

5. ______________________________

Because: ______________________________

____

6. ______________________________

Because: ______________________________

____

7. ______________________________

Because: ______________________________

____

Once you finish, go back and read everything and say to yourself or out loud: "Thank You God for this blessing" after each blessing. Having an attitude of gratitude will attract more to be grateful for in your life.

____ / ____ / ____

COUNT YOUR BLESSINGS!

LIST 7 THINGS YOU ARE *grateful* FOR

Today I A.M. Grateful for

1. ____________________
Because: ____________________

2. ____________________
Because: ____________________

3. ____________________
Because: ____________________

4. ____________________
Because: ____________________

5. ____________________
Because: ____________________

6. ____________________
Because: ____________________

7. ____________________
Because: ____________________

Once you finish, go back and read everything and say to yourself or out loud: "Thank You God for this blessing" after each blessing. Having an attitude of gratitude will attract more to be grateful for in your life.

____ /____ /____

COUNT YOUR BLESSINGS!

LIST 7 THINGS YOU ARE *grateful* FOR

Today I A.M. Grateful for

1. ______________________________

Because: ______________________________

____

2. ______________________________

Because: ______________________________

____

3. ______________________________

Because: ______________________________

____

4. ______________________________

Because: ______________________________

____

5. ______________________________

Because: ______________________________

____

6. ______________________________

Because: ______________________________

____

7. ______________________________

Because: ______________________________

____

Once you finish, go back and read everything and say to yourself or out loud: "Thank You God for this blessing" after each blessing. Having an attitude of gratitude will attract more to be grateful for in your life.

____ /____ /____

COUNT YOUR BLESSINGS!

LIST 7 THINGS YOU ARE *grateful* FOR

Today I A.M. Grateful for

1. ____________________

Because: ____________________

____

2. ____________________

Because: ____________________

____

3. ____________________

Because: ____________________

____

4. ____________________

Because: ____________________

____

5. ____________________

Because: ____________________

____

6. ____________________

Because: ____________________

____

7. ____________________

Because: ____________________

____

Once you finish, go back and read everything and say to yourself or out loud: "Thank You God for this blessing" after each blessing. Having an attitude of gratitude will attract more to be grateful for in your life.

____ / ____ / ____

COUNT YOUR BLESSINGS!

LIST 7 THINGS YOU ARE *grateful* FOR

Today I A.M. Grateful for

1. __________

Because: __________

____

2. __________

Because: __________

____

3. __________

Because: __________

____

4. __________

Because: __________

____

5. __________

Because: __________

____

6. __________

Because: __________

____

7. __________

Because: __________

____

Once you finish, go back and read everything and say to yourself or out loud: "Thank You God for this blessing" after each blessing. Having an attitude of gratitude will attract more to be grateful for in your life.

____ /____ /____

COUNT YOUR BLESSINGS!

LIST 7 THINGS YOU ARE *grateful* FOR

Today I A.M. Grateful for

1. ____________________

Because: ____________________

____

2. ____________________

Because: ____________________

____

3. ____________________

Because: ____________________

____

4. ____________________

Because: ____________________

____

5. ____________________

Because: ____________________

____

6. ____________________

Because: ____________________

____

7. ____________________

Because: ____________________

____

Once you finish, go back and read everything and say to yourself or out loud: "Thank You God for this blessing" after each blessing. Having an attitude of gratitude will attract more to be grateful for in your life.

___ /___ /___

COUNT YOUR BLESSINGS!

LIST 7 THINGS YOU ARE *grateful* FOR

Today I A.M. Grateful for

1. ______________________________

Because: ______________________________

____

2. ______________________________

Because: ______________________________

____

3. ______________________________

Because: ______________________________

____

4. ______________________________

Because: ______________________________

____

5. ______________________________

Because: ______________________________

____

6. ______________________________

Because: ______________________________

____

7. ______________________________

Because: ______________________________

____

Once you finish, go back and read everything and say to yourself or out loud: "Thank You God for this blessing" after each blessing. Having an attitude of gratitude will attract more to be grateful for in your life.

____ / ____ / ____

COUNT YOUR BLESSINGS!

LIST 7 THINGS YOU ARE *grateful* FOR

Today I A.M. Grateful for

1. __________

Because: __________

2. __________

Because: __________

3. __________

Because: __________

4. __________

Because: __________

5. __________

Because: __________

6. __________

Because: __________

7. __________

Because: __________

Once you finish, go back and read everything and say to yourself or out loud: "Thank You God for this blessing" after each blessing. Having an attitude of gratitude will attract more to be grateful for in your life.